AWARDS FOR EXCELLENCE
2010
WINNING PROJECTS

**THEODORE C. THOERIG AND
PATRICK J. PONTIUS**

This book was made possible in part
through the generous sponsorship of

GROSVENOR

Living cities

AWARDS FOR EXCELLENCE

2010

WINNING PROJECTS

Project Staff

Gayle Berens
Senior Vice President
Education and Advisory Group

Adrienne Schmitz
Senior Director, Publications

Theodore C. Thoerig
Manager, Awards and Publications

Patrick J. Pontius
Director, Education and Advisory Group

James A. Mulligan
Managing Editor

Laura Glassman
Publications Professionals LLC
Manuscript Editor

Betsy VanBuskirk
Art Director

Craig Chapman
Senior Director, Publishing Operations

Design and Composition

John Hall Design Group
Beverly, Massachusetts
www.johnhalldesign.com

Jennifer Estrada
Design Assistant

Urban Land Institute
1025 Thomas Jefferson Street, NW
Suite 500 West
Washington, DC 20007-5201

Recommended bibliographic listing:
Thoerig, Theodore C., and Patrick J. Pontius. *Awards for Excellence: 2010 Winning Projects*. Washington, D.C.: Urban Land Institute, 2010.

ULI Catalog number: A28

About the Urban Land Institute

The mission of the Urban Land Institute is to provide leadership in the responsible use of land and in creating and sustaining thriving communities worldwide. ULI is committed to

- Bringing together leaders from across the fields of real estate and land use policy to exchange best practices and serve community needs;
- Fostering collaboration within and beyond ULI's membership through mentoring, dialogue, and problem solving;
- Exploring issues of urbanization, conservation, regeneration, land use, capital formation, and sustainable development;
- Advancing land use policies and design practices that respect the uniqueness of both built and natural environments;
- Sharing knowledge through education, applied research, publishing, and electronic media; and
- Sustaining a diverse global network of local practice and advisory efforts that address current and future challenges.

Established in 1936, the Institute today has more than 28,500 members in over 90 countries, representing the entire spectrum of the land use and development disciplines. ULI relies heavily on the experience of its members. It is through member involvement and information resources that ULI has been able to set standards of excellence in development practice. The Institute has long been recognized as one of the world's most respected and widely quoted sources of objective information on urban planning, growth, and development.

THE ULI AWARDS FOR EXCELLENCE PROGRAM

A guiding principle of the Urban Land Institute is that the achievement of excellence in land use practice should be recognized and rewarded. Since 1979, ULI has honored outstanding development projects in both the private and public sectors with the ULI Awards for Excellence program, which today is widely recognized as the development community's most prestigious awards program. ULI Awards for Excellence recognize the full development process of a project, not just its architecture or design—although these elements play an important role in the overall project. Each award is presented to the development project, with the developer accepting on behalf of the project.

Nominations are open to all, not just ULI members. Juries of ULI full members, chaired by trustees, choose finalists and winners. Jury members represent many fields of real estate development expertise, including finance, land planning, development, public affairs, design, and other professional services. They also represent a broad geographic diversity.

ULI began the Awards for Excellence program in 1979 with the objective of recognizing truly superior development efforts. The criteria for the awards involve factors that go beyond good design, including leadership, contribution to the community, innovations, public/private partnership, environmental protection and enhancement, response to societal needs, and financial success. Winning projects represent the highest standards of achievement in the development industry, standards that ULI members hold worthy of attainment in their professional endeavors. All types of projects have been recognized for their excellence, including office, residential, recreational, urban/mixed use, industrial/office park, commercial/retail, new community, rehabilitation, public, and heritage projects, as well as programs and projects that do not fit into any of these product categories.

For the first three years of the program, only one Award for Excellence was granted each year. In 1982, ULI trustees authorized awards for two winners—one large-scale project and one small-scale project—to recognize excellence regardless of size. Starting in 1985, the awards program shifted emphasis to product categories, while also retaining the small- and large-scale designations. As the program matured, new categories were added to reflect changes in the development industry. In 2002, the last year in which winners were awarded by category, there were 18 categories and up to 11 possible awards.

The Special Award was established in 1986 to acknowledge up to two projects and/or programs that are socially desirable but do not necessarily meet the official awards guidelines governing financial viability, and exemplary projects that are not easily categorized. In 1989, the Heritage Award was introduced to acknowledge projects that have established an industry standard for excellence, and that have been completed for at least 25 years. As of 2010, only ten Heritage Awards have been granted.

When the awards program began, only projects located in the United States or Canada were considered. Beginning with the 1994 awards, ULI's board of trustees authorized the creation of an International Award for a project outside the United States and Canada. With the 2001 awards, the board eliminated this category, opening all categories to all projects, regardless of location.

In 2003, ULI eliminated all category designations, with the exception of the Heritage Award, and did more to recognize the excellence of all the finalist projects in the awards process, not just the award winners. In 2004, ULI inaugurated the ULI Awards for Excellence: Europe, Middle East, and Africa (EMEA, formerly Europe), adopting the same criteria and a similar selection process, and juried by EMEA-based ULI members. And in 2005, the Awards for Excellence program continued to evolve with the introduction of the ULI Awards for Excellence: Asia Pacific.

Also new in 2005 was the introduction of the ULI Global Awards for Excellence. A select jury of international members, charged with choosing up to five Global Award winners from among that year's 20 award-winning projects, announced three global winners in 2005. In each year since, five projects have won Global Awards.

The 2011 "Call for Entries" for the Americas, EMEA, and Asia Pacific competitions is available on the ULI Awards Web page (www.uli.org/AwardsAndCompetitions).

JUDGING CRITERIA

1. Although architectural excellence is certainly a factor, the ULI Awards for Excellence is not a "beauty contest."

2. The project or program must be substantially completed. If the project is phased, the first phase must be completed and operationally stable.

3. No specific age or time constraints apply, except for the Heritage Award (which recognizes projects and/or programs that have been completed for at least 25 years).

4. The project must be financially viable, which means it must be in stable operation and financially successful. An applicant must be able to document the prudent use of financial resources to justify the achievement of a financial return. Programs and projects developed by nonprofit or public agencies are necessarily exempt from the financial viability requirement.

5. The project must demonstrate relevance to the contemporary and future needs of the community in which it is located. The community reaction to the project also is taken into consideration.

6. The project must stand out from others in its category.

7. The project must be an exemplary representative of good development and a model for similar projects worldwide.

SELECTION PROCESS

1. Applications are available as a downloadable document on the ULI Web site's Awards page (www.uli.org/AwardsAndCompetitions).

2. Developers and/or other members of the development team submit completed applications to ULI by a given date in February. Each completed entry must contain the developer's name and signature.

3. The three Awards for Excellence juries—the Americas, EMEA, and Asia Pacific—separately convene to review submissions and choose finalists.

4. At least one jury member visits each finalist project.

5. When all site visits have been completed, the respective juries reconvene to evaluate the finalist projects and choose award winners—up to ten in the Americas, five in EMEA, and five in Asia Pacific. Among all regions, the jury may also choose one Heritage Award winner.

The Americas awards are announced and officially honored at an awards ceremony at ULI's annual Spring Council Forum. The EMEA and Asia Pacific awards are announced at their respective spring or summer conferences. The Global Awards are announced and officially honored at ULI's Fall Meeting.

CONTENTS

PHOTOGRAPHS (FROM TOP TO BOTTOM) BY URBAN REDEVELOPMENT AUTHORITY OF SINGAPORE; MICHAEL O'CALLAHAN; DISTRICT OF COLUMBIA, OFFICE OF PLANNING; FRANCESCO BEDINI; DIXI CARRILLO

As ULI as an organization has become more global, so too have its awards programs. The Institute now has programs that honor projects in all regions of the world—the Americas; Europe, the Middle East, and Africa; and Asia Pacific—as well as the capstone Global Awards for Excellence. In the 32-year history of the Awards for Excellence, 309 projects have been selected as winners, ranging from iconic developments such as Rockefeller Center and the Galleria to small-scale success stories from locales as remote as northwest Pakistan and tsunami-ravaged Sri Lanka.

The Global Awards for Excellence take ULI's best practice standards one step further, identifying the five projects worldwide each year that represent workable, livable, and sustainable models for future development. The global awards jury, composed of industry leaders from around the world, selects projects that not only exhibit high-quality urban design and architecture, but also represent the best cross-regional lessons for all ULI members.

In 2010, ULI received more than 240 applications from around the world. From this pool, 20 projects—from a 5 million-square-foot entertainment district in downtown Los Angeles to a lake restoration project in Bengbu, China—were selected as development models worthy of emulation. Each winner, along with the inaugural winner of the Amanda Burden Urban Open Space Award, is featured in this publication, *Awards for Excellence: 2010 Winning Projects*. Of these 20 winners, five were elevated to global award-winning status; they are presented in the front of the book.

In 2010, the ULI Foundation Governors Endowment Circle was formed to help underwrite the Awards for Excellence program. Foundation Governors are brought into the Endowment Circle when they double their original contribution. Those new funds are then used to support the ULI Awards for Excellence and other recognition programs.

Patrick L. Phillips
Chief Executive Officer
ULI

Richard M. Rosan
Chief Executive Officer
ULI Foundation

AWARDS FOR EXCELLENCE
2010
WINNING PROJECTS

**THEODORE C. THOERIG AND
PATRICK J. PONTIUS**

GLOBAL WINN

ERS

L.A. LIVE

LOS ANGELES, CALIFORNIA

The 27-acre (10.9-ha) L.A. LIVE project has energized downtown Los Angeles by creating a dynamic new hub of activity where Angelenos and tourists can engage in a variety of entertainment opportunities. Located in the South Park area of downtown Los Angeles near the confluence of the 10 and the 110 freeways and in proximity to light rail, L.A. LIVE shines like a beacon and captivates the eye with its sleek, 54-story skyscraper and effervescent LED signage. Offering many options, this sports- and entertainment-oriented development's 5 million square feet (464,500 m²)

DEVELOPMENT TEAM

Owner/Developer
AEG
Los Angeles, California
www.aegworldwide.com

Architects
Gensler
Santa Monica, California
www.gensler.com

RTKL
Los Angeles, California
www.rtkl.com

ELS Architecture and Urban Design
Berkeley, California
www.elsarch.com

JURY STATEMENT

L.A. LIVE, anchored by the STAPLES Center and featuring 5 million square feet of entertainment, hospitality, and office uses, has transformed a stretch of underused land in downtown Los Angeles into a vibrant, 24-hour entertainment district and stimulated the development of more than 2,500 housing units, a grocery store, and dozens of restaurants and cafés in adjacent neighborhoods.

houses two hotels, upscale residences, the STAPLES Center multipurpose arena, the Nokia Theatre, and numerous restaurants, among other uses, and anchors a part of downtown that once sat neglected and forlorn.

The success of L.A. LIVE reflects the culmination of a long and concerted partnership between AEG and the city of Los Angeles. In 1997, hoping to invigorate the city's ailing convention center and the moribund South Park neighborhood, the city of Los Angeles, through its Community Redevelopment Agency, entered into a series of agreements with AEG to develop the STAPLES Center and the surrounding area. The agency was able to condemn and convey to AEG 24 acres (9.7 ha) adjacent to the STAPLES Center site to begin to achieve three public purposes: the construction of a flagship convention hotel, the creation of a sports and entertainment district to support the hotel, and the assembly of space for future expansion of the convention center. The $375 million STAPLES Center, financed

PHOTOGRAPHS BY RYAN GOBUTY (4, 6R, 7);
AEG (5, 6L)

entirely by private funds, opened in 1999 as the start of L.A. LIVE and is the world's most successful arena, attracting more than 240 events and 4 million guests annually.

With the tremendous activity and interest generated by the STAPLES Center, AEG was able to begin the second phase of L.A. LIVE in 2005, opening the 235,000-square-foot (21,800-m²), 7,100-seat Nokia Theatre and 40,000–square-foot (3,700-m²) Nokia Plaza in 2007. Phase III followed shortly thereafter with a pair of major mixed-use buildings along Figueroa Street housing restaurants, a nightclub, the West Coast headquarters for ESPN, and the Grammy Museum. The final phase in 2010 brought a sizable amount of meeting and hotel space as well as the development's signature tower. Housing an 878-room J.W. Marriott hotel, a 123-room Ritz Carlton hotel, and 224 opulent Ritz Residences, the L.A. LIVE tower is the first major skyscraper constructed in downtown Los Angeles in almost 20 years. Both hotels will likely receive LEED certification.

Today, L.A. LIVE is well on its way to enhancing downtown and accomplishing the goals set by the city in 1997. The convention center has seen an 800 percent increase in bookings, and the South Park neighborhood has enjoyed significant investment and now boasts more than 2,500 residents. L.A. LIVE has become a central gathering space for this far-flung metropolis and hosts numerous events ranging from Lakers celebrations to red-carpet premieres. Beyond catalyzing a neighborhood and entertaining tourists and locals alike, L.A. LIVE has generated significant public benefit. AEG negotiated a comprehensive Community Benefits Agreement before commencing construction. This agreement has resulted in almost $6 million for 165 affordable housing units, $1 million for the creation of two parks nearby, and an L.A. LIVE workforce comprising more than 55 percent local residents. The Grammy Museum is the physical manifestation of all of the public art fees generated by L.A. LIVE's construction. The term "downtown Los Angeles" once seemed like an oxymoron to many, but L.A. LIVE has greatly contributed to the reemergence and ever-growing vitality of downtown Los Angeles.

PROJECT DATA

Web Site
www.lalive.com

Site Area
27 ac (10.9 ha)

Facilities
150,000 sf (13,900 m²) office
5 million sf (464,500 m²) retail/
 restaurant/entertainment
224 multifamily units
1,001 hotel rooms
3,500 parking spaces

Land Use
retail, office, restaurant,
 entertainment, hotel, residential,
 parks/open space, sports

Start/Completion Dates
1999–March 2012 (projected)

Miasteczko Wilanów

WARSAW, POLAND

A city shattered during the 20th century by two world wars, Warsaw, over the last two decades, has too often been developed in an exploitative and incoherent manner. Miasteczko Wilanów, a new town for more than 20,000 residents approximately ten kilometers (6 mi) southeast of the city center, is a modern incarnation of the urban typology that Warsaw lost during the last century: a mixed-use, architecturally rich, pedestrian-oriented district. With a planned 240,500 square meters (2.6 million sf) of office, 68,000 square meters (732,000 sf) of retail, and 19,500 residential units underway, the new town has contributed to a rise in land value, from $50 per square meter ($4.65 per sf) to $470 per square meter ($43.66 per sf) in 2010.

JURY STATEMENT

Miasteczko Wilanów—a pedestrian-oriented, architecturally rich new neighborhood in Warsaw—is a return to the urban morphology that was lost to the city in the war-torn 20th century. The 169-hectare mixed-use district is home to more than 20,000 residents and reestablishes sustainable planning and development practices in this rapidly expanding central European metropolis.

DEVELOPMENT TEAM

Developers
Investment Environments
Warsaw, Poland
www.in-vi.com

Prokom Investments SA
Warsaw, Poland

Master Planner
Investment Vision
Warsaw, Poland
www.in-vi.com

The district master plan was inspired by the historical context of the site and the character of the remaining pre–World War I neighborhoods near the center of Warsaw. Originally envisioning a gated residential community, the master planners—Warsaw-based Investment Vision—reversed course, instead working toward an open, inclusive mixed-use plan that incorporates meaningful institutions such as places of worship, schools, and health care facilities. The master plan implemented flexible design guidelines, which resulted in an authentic architectural harmony brought about by the coordinated participation of 20 local architecture firms. New buildings do not strive to be architectural monuments but instead complement the existing institutional buildings, such as the Wilanów Palace and the landmark Catholic church.

The mid-rise district is composed of four- to five-story buildings oriented around central nodes, such as the planned retail town center and a fixture of Polish culture, the local Catholic church. Miasteczko

PHOTOGRAPHS BY GUY PERRY, IN-VI (ALL PHOTOS)

Wilanów's church, known as the Temple of Divine Providence, has special significance in Warsaw. With important cultural figures buried in its catacombs, the church has become the final stop on one of Warsaw's most important processional routes.

Residential buildings are organized as perimeter blocks surrounding an internal courtyard. Offices of similar height and density are situated in a parklike setting along the planned ring road. A town center consisting of four- to six-story buildings with retail on the lower levels and office and residential above is planned for the center of the community.

A central plank of the master plan was to make the new district as pedestrian-friendly as possible. Both the church and the future town center are within a 15-minute walk from any point in the community, shops and basic services are all within a five-minute walk for most residents, and playgrounds are incorporated into virtually every block. Even with a parking ratio of 1.5 spaces per residential unit, more than 85 percent of parking is in underground carparks, often equipped with stacking systems. The rest of the spaces are on the street; the district does not have a single surface lot.

Miasteczko Wilanów has been successful in establishing sustainable planning and development practices in the context of a rapidly expanding central European metropolis. Its emphasis on walkability and mixed use runs contrary to many standard market practices in the region, which usually involve creating single-use districts, gating residential neighborhoods, enclosing retail in shopping malls, and giving priority to automobile access and parking.

PROJECT DATA

Web Site
www.miasteczko-wilanow.pl

Site Area
169 hectares (418 ac)

Facilities
28,500 m² (307,000 sf) office (240,500 m²/2.6 million sf at buildout)
7,000 m² (75,000 sf) retail (68,000 m²/732,000 sf at buildout)
10,900 multifamily units (19,500 at buildout)
250 hotel rooms at buildout
16,350 parking spaces (29,250 at buildout)

Land Uses
residential, office, retail, entertainment, hotel, civic, education, restaurant, parks

Start/Completion Dates
2000–2016 (projected)

Rouse Hill Town Centre

ROUSE HILL, NEW SOUTH WALES, AUSTRALIA

Formerly the site of a golf course, Rouse Hill Town Centre brings 210 shops, 104 residences, 2,800 square meters (30,000 sf) of office space, ten restaurants, a cinema, and multiple educational and civic uses to Rouse Hill, a suburb approximately 40 kilometers (25 mi) northwest of Sydney, Australia. The lifestyle center combines the traditional streetscape of a contemporary town with community spaces and the convenience of the latest shopping, dining, and entertainment options. Launched in March 2008 and developed at a cost of A$470 million, Rouse Hill Town Centre opened fully leased and has won praise for its extensive environmentally friendly features, creating a ripple effect in the Australian retail industry.

JURY STATEMENT

Rouse Hill Town Centre, an ecologically conscious regional shopping center, features more than 210 retailers, 104 apartments, 2,800 square meters of office space, ten restaurants, and a cinema.

DEVELOPMENT TEAM

Owner/Developer
The GPT Group
Sydney, New South Wales, Australia
www.gpt.com.au

Master Planners
Lend Lease Group
Sydney, New South Wales, Australia
www.lendlease.com.au

CIVITAS Urban Design & Planning
Vancouver, British Columbia, Canada
www.civitasdesign.com

Design Architects
Allen Jack + Cottier Architects Pty
  Ltd.
Sydney, New South Wales, Australia
www.architectsajc.com

Rice Daubney
Sydney, New South Wales, Australia
www.ricedaubney.com.au

Group GSA
East Sydney, New South Wales,
  Australia
www.groupgsa.com

Rouse Hill Town Centre sits at the heart of the 120-hectare (297-ac) New Rouse Hill site, an area earmarked for development in the 1980s by the New South Wales (NSW) government. Designating the site as the new regional hub for the rapidly growing northwest suburb of Sydney, the NSW Department of Planning invited bids for development in 2001. The area's market fundamentals were strong: its population of 300,000—already underserved by retail—is estimated to grow at three times the citywide average. In 2003, the GPT Group won the bid to develop the site.

The project's master plan was prepared by a joint venture between Lend Lease and the GPT Group, in partnership with the NSW Department of Planning and the state-owned corporation Landcom. The lifestyle center is organized around the town square, which serves as a central reference point and the locale for civic events. The large-format anchor tenants are situated at the four corners of the 19-hectare (47 ac) site. The density increases along Main Street, where the pedestrian-friendly design mitigates vehicular flow. The town center's 104 residential units and 2,800 square meters (30,000 sf) of office space are atop the ground-floor retail along this central spine. In addition to commercial uses, the Hills Shire Council's Vinegar Hill Memorial Library and Community Centre surround the town square, creating a cultural heart in the community. The majority of the 3,174 parking spaces are located underground.

A pedestrian loop creates an inner ring within the town center, offering an open-air shopping experience protected from the elements. Shades, awnings, and louvers are outfitted with sensors that react to wind, rain, and sun, ensuring protection from the environment while maintaining natural ventilation. "The handling of the relationship between indoor and outdoor, and their apparent seamless transition in many instances, is particularly commendable," says juror Rocco Yim, executive director of Hong Kong's Rocco Design Architects Ltd.

Rouse Hill Town Centre is one of Australia's first regional shopping centers to demonstrate a comprehensive approach to sustainability. After its first year of operation, the complex reduced its ecological footprint by 32 percent compared to a standard NSW regional shopping center. The GPT Group introduced mandatory green leases, requiring its tenants to meet minimum water and energy standards as well as a minimum ecological footprint. The developer uses a number of tools to encourage energy reductions; for instance, a "pay as you go" approach to air conditioning has provided a financial incentive for tenants to use their cooling systems more efficiently. Rainwater captured in a 150,000-liter (39,626-gal) rainwater tank is recycled for use in toilets and irrigation.

PROJECT DATA

Web Site
www.rhtc.com.au

Site Area
19 hectares (47 ac)

Facilities
2,800 m² (30,000 sf) office
66,200 m² (713,000 sf) retail
104 multifamily units
3,174 parking spaces

Land Uses
retail, residential, office, restaurants, entertainment, education, civic, open space, surface parking

Start/Completion Dates
April 2006–March 2008

Southern Ridges

SINGAPORE

With 4.9 million people sharing 710 square kilometers (274 sq mi)—most of it heavily urbanized—Singapore is one of the most densely populated countries in the world. The Singapore government faces a challenge in maintaining high quality of life and offering suitable recreational opportunities in this increasingly dense environment. At Southern Ridges—a nine-kilometer (5.6-mi) chain of open spaces connecting three existing hill parks—the Urban Redevelopment Authority (URA) of Singapore has managed to create a contiguous nature preserve in an environment with limited open space.

Southern Ridges connects three existing parks—Mount Faber Park, Telok Blangah Hill Park, and Kent Ridge Park—which had been separated by major arterial roads and dense vegetation. Each park was notable on its own, but they were not easily accessible. The design concept, therefore, was to link these open spaces with a series of pedestrian bridges and walkways, creating one large natural preserve. Given the fragile environment, the URA made unobtrusive and ecologically sensitive design a priority when it selected architects through an international design competition in 2003.

DEVELOPMENT TEAM

Owner
Ministry of National Development
Singapore
www.mnd.gov.sg

Developer/Master Planner
Urban Redevelopment Authority
Singapore
www.ura.gov.sg

**Design Architects
(Henderson Waves)**
RSP Architects Planners &
  Engineers (Pte) Ltd.
Singapore
www.rsp.com.sg

IJP Corporation Architects
London, United Kingdom
www.ijpcorporation.com

**Design Architect (Alexandra Arch
and Forest Walk)**
LOOK Architects
Singapore
www.lookarchitects.com

Design Architect (HortPark)
MKPL Architects Pte Ltd.
Singapore
www.mkpl.sg

JURY STATEMENT

The Southern Ridges is a nine-kilometer chain of open spaces that connects the rolling hills of three existing parks. The project, visited by a half million people since its opening, creates a rare contiguous recreational space in densely populated Singapore.

The three most popular elements of the park system are the bridges—Henderson Waves and Alexandra Arch—and the elevated pathway, the Forest Walk. Located 36 meters (118 ft) above Henderson Road, the torqued Henderson Waves bridge spans 274 meters (899 ft) connecting two hill parks. The bridge's wavelike form—designed by local firm RSP Architects Planners & Engineers and London-based IJP Corporation Architects—was based on the mathematical concept of periodicity, which is the same equation that governs the oscillation of ocean or sound waves. The bridge's largest wave, 57 meters long (187 ft) and six meters high (20 ft) at its crest, is centered above the main road. The bridge's walkway is made of yellow balau timber, which softens the bridge's appearance. Seating and alcoves for visitors are located along the walkway.

Forest Walk, designed by locally based LOOK Architects, is an elevated walkway that guides park users up the steep, forested terrain of Telok Blangah Hill. The 1.3-kilometer (0.8-mi) walkway traverses the terrain in a switchback fashion, offering views of the forest, city, and coastline below. The walkways are constructed from a thin mesh of structural steel, permitting sunlight to penetrate to the forest floor and preventing the retention of rainwater. The strength of the material also allowed the designers to use of less of it, reducing the overall impact, both visual and actual, on the sensitive environment.

The Alexandra Arch draws its inspiration from the form of a folded leaf. It serves as the "gateway to nature," leading visitors into the Forest Walk. The asymmetric bridge has a tilted arch, rising six meters (20 ft) above Alexandra Road and spanning 80 meters (262 ft). The ribbed arch is illuminated at night using color-changing LED lights, with a programmed display meant to simulate dusk in the tropics.

The Alexandra Arch allows visitors to walk from Telok Blagah Hill Park to the 23 hectares (57 ac) of lawns and gardens at the horticulture park (HortPark). The park's Visitor Centre, designed by local firm MKPL Architects, is a U-shaped complex, with 255 square meters (2,749 sf) of office space and 178 square meters (1,911 sf) of retail area surrounding a courtyard of athletic fields and gardens.

Since its opening in May 2008, Southern Ridges has been visited by more than a half-million people, averaging 6,000 visitors on the weekends and 35,000 each month. The project is another link in URA's plans to connect the hill parks to the waterfront along the southern coastline of Singapore. When that project is completed in 2012, URA will have created a comprehensive recreational loop, allowing visitors to experience each of Singapore's distinct ecological zones, from dense forests to mangrove trails to beaches.

PROJECT DATA

Web Site
www.ura.gov.sg/sr_bridges

Site Area
10 hectares (24.7 ac)

Land Uses
park, open space

Start/Completion Dates
November 2002–May 2008

Thin Flats

PHILADELPHIA, PENNSYLVANIA

Located among the rowhouses of Philadelphia's Northern Liberties neighborhood, the eight-unit Thin Flats lives up to its name: each of the two-story units, stacked in pairs, is only 18 feet (5.5 m) wide. Developed by Onion Flats, a family-run Philadelphia-based firm, the new stacked duplexes are a rethinking of the traditional Philadelphia rowhouse—usually a long, narrow, light-deficient typology. The LEED-Platinum project uses light wells to brighten the core of the units, solar panels to provide domestic hot water, green roofing to decrease thermal gain, and rainwater-

JURY STATEMENT

Certified LEED for Homes Platinum, Thin Flats is an eight-unit infill development in north Philadelphia that uses solar water heating, a green roof, and rainwater harvesting to reduce energy and water consumption by an estimated 50 percent. This prototype is now being scaled up for use in other cities, emerging as a develop/design/build model that is replicable for infill sites across the country and even around the world.

DEVELOPMENT TEAM

Owner/Developer
Onion Flats, LLC
Philadelphia, Pennsylvania
www.onionflats.com

Design Architect
Plumbob, LLC
Philadelphia, Pennsylvania
www.onionflats.com

harvesting cisterns for irrigation of yards and gardens. The *Philadelphia Inquirer* declared that this blend of environmental and design sensibility "makes Thin Flats easily the most exciting rowhouse project to come out of Philadelphia's recent construction boom."

In 1997, two brothers, Tim and Pat McDonald—an architect and contractor, respectively— purchased a 200-year-old, five-story former meatpacking plant in the Old City section of Philadelphia with the intention of creating a living laboratory for the family to work together. By 2001, the building had been transformed into Capital Flats, an eight-unit loft project with an architecture studio below. Almost by accident, a develop/design/build collective had emerged—one that can control every aspect of a project's development and management, from initial concept to kitchen finishes.

Onion Flats has concentrated its efforts in Northern Liberties, a depressed community of red-brick rowhouses and light-industrial uses. Despite its condition, the neighborhood was dense, mixed use, walkable, and close to transit, which all provide for an attractive lifestyle that does not require a car. The firm began purchasing vacant lots and buildings in the neighborhood in 1999 and 2000. Thin Flats, started in September 2007, required the assembly of nine vacant parcels on Laurel Street.

The neighborhood's dominant residential form, the rowhouse, with its vertical rhythm and regularity, was the main design inspiration for Thin Flats. Facing the street, the building presents a complex double facade: an irregular composition of glass and metal panels punctuated with openings stands three feet (1 m) in front of an inner facade, creating an entry space, a sense of depth, and a chimney effect that draws hot air up and away from the units. The variegated street wall stands in stark contrast to the traditional brick rowhouses on either side.

The energy and water savings at Thin Flats are significant: the project uses approximately 50 percent less energy—and 71 percent less energy for heating—than a comparable building, as well as reducing water consumption by 50 percent. The top of the building supports both an intensive green roof—one

PHOTOGRAPHS BY SAM OBERTER (20, 23); MARIKO REED (21L, 21R); TIM MCDONALD (22L, 22R)

designed to be a natural landscape, requiring a deep soil base—and solar thermal panels, which provide 100 percent of the units' hot water. The green roof plantings meander around hardscaped patios and the numerous skylights, which along with open internal layouts, and interior glass walls and staircases allow natural light to penetrate throughout. Two cisterns capture rainwater that filters through the pervious pavement system in the parking area for use in irrigation. A heat-recovery ventilation system improves indoor air quality, and a central, automated monitoring system increases efficiency to reduce lighting and overall energy costs. Often, green building accreditation requires materials to be sourced within a 500-mile (800-km) radius; at Thin Flats, materials came from suppliers within a five-mile (8-km) range.

The Thin Flats prototype is now being scaled up for use in other cities, emerging as a develop/design/build model that is replicable for infill sites across the country and even worldwide. In fact, Onion Flats already has begun experimenting with different production modes, working to break down a building like Thin Flats into modular units that can be reassembled on site.

PROJECT DATA

Web Site
thinflats.leedphilly.com

Site Area
0.38 acre (0.15 ha)

Facilities
8 multifamily units
8 parking spaces

Land Use
residential, surface parking

Start/Completion Dates
September 2007–February 2009

COMMERC

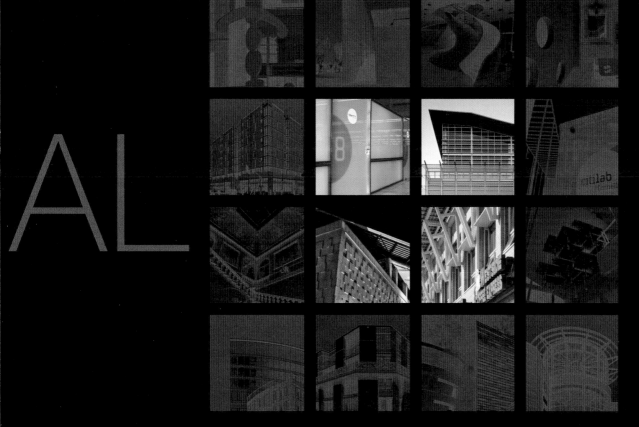

AL

Bethel Commercial Center

CHICAGO, ILLINOIS

Bethel Commercial Center is a mixed-use transit-oriented commercial center adjacent to a Green Line "L" station in a low-income neighborhood on Chicago's west side. The 22,000-square-foot (2,044-m²) center includes ground-floor retail space, employment and job-training offices, a bank—the only full-service one in the neighborhood—and a daycare center, allowing residents to drop off and pick up children and to get to and from work, all without the use of a car. The building, which uses approximately 50 percent less energy than conventional construction, achieved a LEED-Gold rating in 2008.

JURY STATEMENT

Arising out of a community effort to activate development along the Green Line train route serving Chicago's West Garfield neighborhood, Bethel Commercial Center houses ground-floor retail space, employment and job-training offices, the only full-service bank in the neighborhood, and a daycare center, allowing residents to drop off and pick up children and commute to and from work, all without the use of a car.

DEVELOPMENT TEAM

Owner/Developer
Bethel New Life
Chicago, Illinois
www.bethelnewlife.org

Design Architect
Farr Associates
Chicago, Illinois
www.farrside.com

The idea for Bethel Commercial Center developed in the late 1990s from a community response to save the Green Line train route, which serves Chicago's West Garfield neighborhood. The community, where only 6 percent of residents own cars, had lost more than 60 percent of its residents since 1960; of those who remained, approximately one-third had incomes below the poverty line. The potential closure of the Lake/Pulaski "L" station and entire Green Line threatened to sever the already isolated neighborhood from downtown employment opportunities.

Bethel New Life, a community development corporation affiliated with West Garfield's historic Bethel Lutheran Church, recognized the threat posed to the neighborhood by the planned closure. Having built more than 1,000 residential units and rehabilitated an old hospital, Bethel New Life was already invested in the community and formulated the Lake Pulaski Transit Village Plan to prove the viability of the station and line. The plan called for affordable, energy-efficient homes, commercial development, and expanded parks and greenways. At the center of the plan was the proposed Bethel Commercial Center, where new jobs, improved transportation, and affordable child care would come together.

The plan worked. Rather than close the elevated train line, the Chicago Transit Authority announced it would renovate the station as part of a $300 million upgrade to the Green Line. The public improvements catalyzed the revitalization, jump-starting the redevelopment of the West Garfield neighborhood. The linchpin of this resurgence was the two-story Bethel Commercial

Center, which sits on the north side of the Lake/Pulaski station and connects directly to the station by a bridge.

The second level of Bethel Commercial Center combines an employment services office, which provides job counseling and placement, with the Community Technology Center, which offers computer and Internet training. It also houses the child care facilities, which provide affordable child care to parents who work or attend school. On the ground floor are six retail spaces, occupied by a sandwich shop, an attorney's office, two nonprofit foundations, a child development facility, and the neighborhood's only bank, offering residents an alternative to payday lending and check-cashing establishments.

In addition to promoting economic and social stability in the neighborhood, Bethel Commercial Center was designed to be sustainable. The brownfield project uses water-efficient landscaping and low-flow plumbing fixtures to cut water use by approximately 30 percent. A green roof absorbs stormwater, reducing the amount of runoff reaching the city sewer system. Two photovoltaic systems—a 25-kilowatt roof tile array and a 6.6-kilowatt awning system—provide approximately 11 percent of the building's power, and the green roof and high-thermal-mass insulation limit temperature fluctuations throughout the day, reducing heating and cooling loads.

The financing for the $4.9 million project, somewhat complicated by the incorporation of green technologies, was funded through a mix of grants and new market tax credits.

Bethel Commercial Center has spurred new development in the neighborhood, including more than 100 affordable housing units, a new park, and a planned grocery store. "The Bethel Commercial Center is the anchor of a larger commitment to activate redevelopment along the Green Line," according to Stacey Flint, senior director, real estate development for Bethel New Life.

PROJECT DATA

Web Site
http://www.farrside.
  com/RoomToRegion.
  aspx?cat=2&sub=1&id=1

Site Area
0.53 acres (0.21 ha)

Facilities
22,000 sf (2,044 m²) commercial

Land Use
office, retail, education, restaurant

Start/Completion Dates
May 2003–August 2005

Citilab

BARCELONA, SPAIN

Located in Cornellà de Llobregat, on the outskirts of Barcelona, Citilab is an adaptive use project that has employed a creative business model to bring new life to a dilapidated industrial area. First conceived in 1997 as part of the local government's plans to preserve the region's industrial fabric, Citilab opened in 2007 with a focus on social and digital innovation. The 5,000 square meters (54,000 sf) of space housed within the 110-year-old former textile factory accom-

JURY STATEMENT

Citilab, a 5,000-square-meter center for social digital innovation near Barcelona, is based in a renovated textile factory that was abandoned after the country's last industrial crisis. In the center of a neighborhood undergoing major urban renewal, Citilab operates as a combination training center, and business and social incubator, leasing space to local startup companies, entrepreneurs, and community associations.

DEVELOPMENT TEAM

Developer
Fundació Privada pel a la foment de
   la Societat del Coneixement
Barcelona, Spain
http://citilab.eu/fundacio

Owner
Ajuntament de Cornellà de Llobregat
Barcelona, Spain

Architects
Julia Arquitectes Associats, S.L.
Barcelona, Spain

modate a conference and training center, a research center, and an incubator for business and social initiatives. The developer, Fundació Privada pel a la foment de la Societat del Coneixement, completed Citilab within budget.

The site is located to the west of the city, about nine kilometers (5.5 mi) north of the international airport and the port of Barcelona. It is accessible by subway with the Cornellà station located less than a ten-minute walk or short tram connection from the site.

PHOTOGRAPHS BY ISIDOR FERNÁNDEZ (30, 32, 33R); TONI DOPICO (31R); JOSÉ IRÚN (31L, 33L)

The exterior of the orange brick Can Suris factory building was preserved and updated with glass awnings along the front roofline. Interior spaces make use of large open areas, wood flooring, and vaulted brick ceilings with raw beams, to evoke the industrial feel of the original building but with a polished modern appeal.

The guiding principle for Citilab began with the idea that digital technologies, especially the Internet, have changed the rules and created new opportunities for innovation and civic engagement. With the Internet as a platform for innovation, Citilab examines the digital effect on creative thinking and concentrates on how citizens and cities can collaborate and use the Internet to improve and strengthen communities. Citilab is organized into five areas: Cities and Citizens; Education and Learning Environments; Social and Economic Impact; Design and Innovation Processes; and Social Media Lab. Approximately 994 square meters (10,700 sf) of the facility is leased to local startup companies, and an equal amount of space is dedicated to local entrepreneurs and community associations. Intergenerational learning is emphasized, and the ground-floor training center features a learning lab for children and one for retirees, along with business uses.

Although promoted by the government, Citilab is economically sustainable and does not require any government subsidy. It has succeeded on multiple levels and offers an effective model of adaptive use of industrial buildings combined with a creative business model. The project has helped members of all ages in the local community, from youth to budding entrepreneurs, embrace technology by providing the technological and physical environment to facilitate learning and development. As one juror stated, "[Citilab] is creative in the way it works with challenges and in producing a project that carries history into the future. Such projects set an example for other important landmarks; restoration projects with an important social impact like this one should be encouraged."

PROJECT DATA

Web Site
http://citilab.eu

Site Area
0.25 ha (0.61 ac)

Facilities
4,800 m² (51,700 sf) office
200 m² (2,152 sf) retail/restaurant/
    entertainment

Land Use
civic, education, research,
    restaurant, office

Start/Completion Dates
May 2005–July 2007

Foundry Square

SAN FRANCISCO, CALIFORNIA

Located in San Francisco's South of Market (SOMA) neighborhood, Foundry Square offers a compelling example of a how a multiblock, mixed-use urban campus can go a long way toward enhancing urban vitality. One of the first developments to transform the urban fabric of the SOMA neighborhood, Foundry Square has been a game changer. It currently consists of four corner parcels, three structures (with a fourth in preconstruction planning), and a dynamic open space at the intersection of First Street and Howard Street. Upon completion, Foundry Square will include 1.6 million square feet (111,500 m²) of office and retail space spread across four mid-rise buildings. The thoughtful design of Foundry Square, from the pioneering incorporation of sustainable

JURY STATEMENT

Foundry Square, a 1.6 million-square-foot, four-building office development in San Francisco, has led the transformation of the Transbay Transit Center District. The mid-rise development's large public spaces and human-scale architecture have activated the streets, and its nontraditional form and floor plate configurations have attracted a variety of high-end tenants.

DEVELOPMENT TEAM

Owner/Developer
Wilson Meany Sullivan
San Francisco, California
www.wmspartners.com

Master Planner/Design Architect
STUDIOS Architecture
San Francisco, California
www.studiosarchitecture.com

Landscape Architect
SWA Group
Sausalito, California
www.swagroup.com

PROJECT DATA

Web Site
Foundry II: www.orrickbuilding.com
Foundry III: www.foundrythree.com
Foundry IV: www.cottonwoodpartners.
   com

Site Area
4.5 ac (1.82 ha)

Facilities
1.0 million sf/95,005 m² office (1.3
   million sf/118,266 m² at buildout)
36,973 sf/3,435 m² retail (46,393
   sf/4,310 m² at buildout)
528 parking spaces (628 at buildout)

Land Use
office, retail, restaurant, open space

Start/Completion Dates
1999–2011 (projected)

technologies to the large open space that activates the street, is what sets it apart from so many other mixed-use developments and makes it a vital contributor to SOMA's revitalization.

Now renowned as a hip area full of lofts and businesses, the SOMA neighborhood is also the future home of the Transbay Transit Center and a Cesar Pelli–designed skyscraper that will change the city's skyline. Yet as recently as a decade ago, this was a neighborhood in decline. In comparison to much of the rest of the city, SOMA historically has lacked architectural character and an active, pedestrian streetscape. Initiated in 1999, Foundry Square opened in 2002 with the completion of Foundry II, now known as the Orrick Building. Foundry IV followed shortly thereafter in 2003. Five years later, in 2008, Foundry I opened. Foundry III, which will complete the development, just received its approvals and construction should soon commence.

Although completion of the four buildings will span a decade, each structure shares a cohesive architectural identity that unifies the Foundry Square complex. All three existing buildings as well as the plans for Foundry III incorporate sustainable design techniques and employ a variety of high-quality materials and architectural details. The buildings feature extensive use of stone and glass, eighth-floor setbacks, and undulating roofs that have enlivened the SOMA skyline. Foundry Square was one of the first commercial mid-rise developments in the United States to focus on sustainability. Some of its features include a ventilated double-wall/air-cavity curtain-wall system and a full, under-floor heating, ventilating, and air-conditioning system. Foundry III is slated to achieve LEED-Platinum certification.

Among the many effective design elements, perhaps the most significant has been the creation of the large open space that embraces all four corners of Foundry Square at Howard and First streets.

PHOTOGRAPHS BY TIM GRIFFITH (34, 36); MICHAEL O'CALLAHAN (35, 37)

Each building features a landscaped entry plaza facing a common intersection, and collectively, these four plazas function as a public space 200 by 200 feet (60 by 60 m). Howard Street has traditionally operated as a major thoroughfare into the city for commuters traveling via the Bay Bridge, and Foundry Square's plaza has created a much-needed pedestrian space that has calmed this heavy traffic.

In addition to being so visually compelling, the design has resulted in a functional space with high market demand. The floor plates are nontraditional and give the tenants tremendous leeway in terms of configuration, whether they prefer open workspaces or private offices. Foundry I, II, and IV enjoy close to 100 percent occupancy with long-term tenants such as Orrick, Herrington & Sutcliffe, BlackRock, Moody's, Barclays Global Investors, and Gymboree. Demand for space in the planned Foundry III will also likely be high because of the continuation of excellent, functional, and sustainable design elements that make Foundry Square such an attractive piece of the SOMA streetscape and an optimal place for productivity.

Greenbelt 5

MAKATI CITY, PHILIPPINES

DEVELOPMENT TEAM

Owner/Developer/Architect
Ayala Land, Inc.
Makati City, Philippines
www.ayalaland.com.ph

Greenbelt 5 is the most recent phase in the continuing development of Greenbelt, a flagship lifestyle center in Makati City, Manila's central business district. Developed and designed by Manila-based Ayala Land, the four-level, 48,680-square-meter (523,987-sf) Greenbelt 5 is sensitive to the traditions of the Philippines, showcasing the country's best designers and products. In addition to upscale shopping options, the new retail center preserves two cultural landmarks and offers open spaces for public events in the adjoining Greenbelt Park.

Adjacent to, and southeast of, Manila, Makati City is the Philippines national capital region's financial and commercial center. Ayala Land, the Philippines' largest developer of retail, office, and multifamily properties, as well as land developer of residential subdivisions, has been building the 37-hectare

JURY STATEMENT

Greenbelt 5 is the latest phase in the continuing development of Greenbelt, a lifestyle center located in Manila's central business district. The new, four-level, 48,680-square-meter shopping center highlights the best the Philippines has to offer in terms of art, architecture, and design alongside upscale retail shops.

(91-ac) Ayala Center in Makati City since 1963. The initial 34 hectares (84 ac) was built as Glorietta, a one-stop super-regional center. Renovated in 2001, the complex reopened with Greenbelt 1, 2, and 3 in 2002; the fourth and fifth phases opened in 2004 and 2007, respectively.

Building on the successful elements of its predecessors, Greenbelt 5 capitalizes on expansive open space, offering al fresco dining, lush gardens, and landscaped pedestrian paths. Taking advantage of the surrounding parks, the interiors of the shopping center feature high ceilings and expansive glass panels that bring the outdoors inside. Greenbelt 5's bridge ways and pedestrian paths are integrated into the central business district's pedestrian system, improving connectivity with nearby residential and office buildings and drawing customers into its shops. Much of the expanded park ground sits atop the structured parking lots.

The facade's metal grillwork is textured to evoke woven textiles, a nod to the long heritage of Filipino weaving. In particular, the facade that faces Greenbelt Park was inspired by a fabric woven by the T'boli, an indigenous people of southern Mindanao. Much of the interior design has a distinctly Filipino flavor, and an entire section, the Filipino zone, is devoted to local design and materials. Divider panels between shops and railings have a pattern inspired by native bamboo, and a variety of local woods are used throughout. Striving to represent more to the community than just a shopping experience, Greenbelt 5 set aside space for art exhibitions and performances in an area with terraces inspired by the rice fields of the north. Greenbelt 5 also preserved existing cultural institutions, integrating the nearby Ayala Museum and a chapel into the plan.

Greenbelt 5 successfully combines distinctly Filipino design and retailers with high-end international brands. The project's creation of a new facade along what had been the back entrance to Greenbelt has reinvigorated development and revitalization of the immediate area. The project has improved the retail tenant mix, resulting in a more than 40 percent increase in foot traffic in all areas of the shopping complex. Greenbelt now commands premium rents, generally 20 to 25 percent above the industry standard. "Greenbelt 5 advances the quality and innovation of retail centers in the Philippines and is a reference for retail center developers in Asia," commented juror Paul Husband, managing director of Husband Retail Consulting in Hong Kong.

Web Site
www.ayalamalls.com.ph

Site Area
7.8 ha (19.3 ac)

Facilities
48,680 m² (523,987 sf) retail

Land Use
retail, restaurant, entertainment,
  parking

Start/Completion Dates
January 2006–October 2008

MIXED U

SE

Andares

ZAPOPAN, JALISCO, MEXICO

Andares is a retail-led mixed-use project comprising a linear, 197-store shopping center; nine apartment towers; two office buildings; and plans for a luxury hotel. Located in Zapopan, a northwest suburb of Guadalajara—Mexico's second-largest city—Andares is one of the largest shopping centers in western Mexico and represents the largest private investment in the country in 2009. Developed by Desarrolladora Mexicana de Inmuebles, S.A., the $320 million lifestyle center mixes luxury retail and residences amid more than two hectares (5 ac) of open spaces, plazas, water mirrors, and gardens.

JURY STATEMENT

Andares, a retail-led mixed-use project comprising a 197-store shopping center, nine apartment towers, two office buildings, and a planned luxury hotel, stands as one of the largest shopping centers in western Mexico and represents the largest private investment in the country in 2009.

DEVELOPMENT TEAM

Owner/Developer
Desarrolladora Mexicana de
  Inmuebles, S.A.
Guadalajara, Mexico

Master Planner/Design Architect
Sordo Madaleno y Asociados
Mexico City, Mexico

Zapopan is home to many wealthy residential neighborhoods: 65 percent of the households with the highest purchasing power in Guadalajara are located in a ten-kilometer (6.2-mi) radius around Andares. The development is situated at the intersection of two major roads and adjacent to Puerta de Hierro, one of the most exclusive residential complexes in the city.

Designed by Mexican architect Javier Sordo Madaleno, Andares combines traditional Mexican techniques and materials with a contemporary, minimalist aesthetic. The project is arranged around two

PHOTOGRAPHS BY FRANCISCO PÉREZ ARRIAGA (ALL IMAGES)

retail spines: the broad Andares Boulevard and the linear interior garden. The 5,000-square-meter (53,800-sf) boulevard, lined with fountains, sculptures, and gardens, is the main entrance to the shopping center, creating a quiet interior street that contrasts with the busy arterial roads that ring the 13.3-hectare (32.9-ac) site. At the terminus of the boulevard stands the 187-unit apartment complex. The nine towers, which include apartments of 100, 160, and 210 square meters (1,080, 1,720, and 2,260 sf) along with 11 penthouses, are connected by a walkway directly to the shopping center.

The rectilinear interior garden's 3,733 square meters (40,182 sf) are landscaped with native plants and surrounded by two levels of open-air retail. The interior shopping complex includes luxury anchors such as Liverpool and Palacio de Hierro, along with a movie theater, casino, and children's entertainment area. The lifestyle center's retail spaces are 95 percent occupied, and more than 45 percent of the stores are new to the region. The retail portion of the project is divided into two main areas: the exclusive Paseo Andares VIP and the interior mall.

In the southwest corner of the project area, Andares includes a business center featuring 27,669 square meters (297,827 sf) of office space. Originally planned for the second phase of Andares, the construction of the office buildings proceeded ahead of schedule based on the success of the shopping complex. A luxury hotel, combined with residences, is planned for the second phase.

The developers also constructed a water treatment plant and an electric substation, creating key city infrastructure for the metropolitan area. The $7.5 million substation has the capacity to supply energy to more than 12,000 homes, and the new water treatment plant reduces the development's effect on the environment by reusing water for landscaping irrigation. At Andares, a central computerized system controls the lighting and water features for optimal energy efficiency and water consumption. The lifestyle center won the 2009 ICSC Latin American Shopping Center gold award in the categories of sustainable design, best design, and innovative development.

PROJECT DATA

Web Site
www.andares.com

Site Area
13.3 ha (32.9 ac)

Facilities
27,669 m² (297,827 sf) office
  (38,000 m²/409,029 sf at buildout)
347,352 m² (3.7 million sf) retail
187 multifamily units
120 hotel rooms (at buildout)
440 parking spaces

Land Use
retail, office, residential, hotel,
  restaurant, parking

Start/Completion Dates
December 2006–October 2012
  (projected)

Columbia Heights Redevelopment

WASHINGTON, D.C.

Once one of Washington's most desirable neighborhoods, Columbia Heights languished without investment for decades after the riots sparked by the assassination of the Rev. Dr. Martin Luther King, Jr., in 1968. For years, buildings remained boarded up, large vacant parcels lay fallow, and efforts to revitalize the neighborhood were unsuccessful. Still, the neighborhood possessed notable buildings and a dense population base. The completion of the Columbia Heights

JURY STATEMENT

Arising from a city-led initiative to revitalize a neighborhood destroyed in the riots following the assassination of the Rev. Martin Luther King, Jr., Columbia Heights features 1.2 million square feet of new development, including more than 600 housing units, 650,000 square feet of large-format and community retail, and refurbished cultural and public spaces.

DEVELOPMENT TEAM

City Agency
Government of the District of
  Columbia, Office of Planning
Washington, D.C.
www.planning.dc.gov/planning

Metrorail Station in 1999 became a watershed event for the community, creating the public infrastructure necessary for private investment. That and other actions by the District of Columbia government spurred much of the regeneration to follow. Today, the community boasts 1.2 million square feet (111,500 m²) of development, including more than 600 housing units, 650,000 square feet (60,400 m²) of retail, 24,000 square feet (2,200 m²) of office space, and a core of cultural and educational institutions.

Because the city government owned several large parcels acquired through eminent domain after the riots, it was able to control the redevelopment of Columbia Heights through the National Capital Revitalization Corporation, a public development company responsible for spurring revitalization in the city's emerging neighborhoods. The city's revitalization initiative hinged on the construction of the Metrorail station in 1999. Within seven years of its opening, Columbia Heights experienced a rapid upswing in fortunes: the average household income had risen from $50,023 in 1999 to $66,526 in 2006; median home values increased from $240,287 to $374,468 in the same period. Although the neighborhood has seen the development of high-priced residential condominiums and townhomes, it still remains one of the city's most economically and ethnically diverse areas.

DC USA, a 540,000-square-foot (50,168-m²), three-level, large-format retail complex anchored by Washington, D.C.'s first Target, is the focal point of the area's commercial core. The shopping center weaves together both large- and small-format stores housing a strong mix of national, regional, and local tenants. DC USA fronts on 14th Street, the neighborhood's main corridor, diagonally across from the historic Tivoli Theater—now Tivoli Square, recently redeveloped as a commercial and entertainment complex. With its historic, Mediterranean-inspired facade preserved, Tivoli Square now accommodates four floors of office space, street-level retail, and a theater.

The neighborhood has added 670 new residential units, including 572 units housed in a quartet of buildings designed by Torti Gallas and Partners: Park Triangle, Kenyon Square, Victory Heights, and

PHOTOGRAPHS BY STEVE HALL/HEDRICH BLESSING (48, 49R, 50L, 50R); JEFFREY TOTARO PHOTOGRAPHY (51); (DISTRICT OF COLUMBIA, OFFICE OF PLANNING (49L)

Highland Park. Residential buildings are set back from the street, creating continuous stretches of ground-floor retail and space for patio dining along the major commercial corridors. The revitalization also includes a focus on culture and arts, with the Dance Institute of Washington, the GALA Hispanic Theatre, and a new civic plaza used for a farmers market and community-based events, as well as community service organizations such as the Greater Washington Urban League and the Latin American Youth Center.

The public/private partnership that fueled the resurgence of Columbia Heights also created enormous economic benefits. More than 1,200 jobs have been generated and more than $12 million in annual tax revenue—up from zero revenue previously—is anticipated. Commercial spaces in the neighborhood are 95 percent leased with a high-quality mix of tenants. Additionally, the land values surrounding the Metro station have more than doubled, even increasing in value during the recent economic downturn. Metrorail ridership is up more than 300 percent at the Columbia Heights station since the opening of DC USA's stores, some of which are among the best-performing locations in their respective chains.

PROJECT DATA

Web Site
www.columbiaheightsnews.org

Site Area
20 acres (8.1 ha)

Facilities
24,000 sf (2,200 m²) office
650,000 sf (60,400 m²) retail
18 single-family units
612 multifamily units
1,820 parking spaces

Land Use
retail, residential, office,
  entertainment, education,
  restaurants, open space

Start/Completion Dates
May 2003–February 2008

Sundance Square

FORT WORTH, TEXAS

Located in the heart of downtown Fort Worth, Sundance Square is a 38-block commercial, residential, and entertainment district that is a paragon of successful, long-term downtown master planning and revitalization. Through a lasting partnership that began in the 1980s and continues today, Sundance Square Management and David M. Schwarz Architects, with frequent input and support from local property owners and the city, have created and adhered to an ambitious master plan that has enlivened downtown Fort Worth. Developer Ed Bass, a key visionary behind Sundance Square, noted that "we have always believed, from the time we started with the restoration of

JURY STATEMENT

The culmination of a 25-year development process, Sundance Square is a 38-block mixed-use district in the heart of Fort Worth that has used pedestrian-friendly design to regenerate the downtown and stem suburban flight. The deliberate development process has created both economic stability—the district is outperforming local, regional, and national real estate markets—and an authenticity driven by extensive historic preservation efforts.

DEVELOPMENT TEAM

Owner/Developer
Sundance Square Management
Fort Worth, Texas
www.sundancesquaremanagement.
com

Master Planner/Design Architect
David M. Schwarz Architects
Washington, D.C.
www.dmsas.com

the initial two-block area in the early 1980s, to today with 20 redeveloped blocks, that Sundance Square is both a financial investment and an investment in the future of our hometown.... I am proud that our generation is giving the next a healthy, vibrant downtown to enjoy and work with going forward."

In the early 1980s, Fort Worth, like most U.S. cities, suffered from a rapidly declining downtown. Suburban flight had siphoned off much of the commercial and retail activity, and the scant development that had occurred had marred the urban fabric. Large, multiblock parking decks and surface parking lots interrupted the downtown street grid and created an unwelcome streetscape for pedestrians. To stem the decline and reposition downtown as a vital urban center, city leaders and local property owners assembled and engaged in an ambitious master-planning process that encompassed 150 city blocks. During the planning process, the group made a strategic decision to concentrate on a 38-block area in the downtown core and designated it as Sundance Square in homage to the legendary Sundance Kid. Sundance Square Management, a private sector firm led by Ed Bass, was tasked with coordinating the master plan.

Sundance Square Management partnered with David M. Schwarz Architects and began working to achieve the master plan's long-term goal of revitalizing downtown by bringing back a mix of residential, commercial, entertainment, and cultural uses to the city center that would generate activity at all hours of the day. What really set the master plan apart was its slow growth approach to development that focused on the city's best interests over a long time horizon. Many cities in the 1980s pursued one massive "downtown savior" project after another, but Sundance Square relied upon a conservative, long-term strategy that would knit the downtown fabric together piece by piece and year by year.

Sundance Square's first triumph occurred in 1991 with the opening of Sundance West, at Third and Stockton streets. This mixed-use development brought new residential, retail, office, and restaurant development to the market, and it included the first cinema in Fort Worth in 50 years. The conversion of the Sanger Department Store building into residential lofts soon followed, and by the early 1990s, downtown enjoyed a burgeoning residential population. These initial phases provided a momentous start to achieving Sundance Square's master plan goals by improving the pedestrian streetscape, restoring historic facades, and filling in holes in the urban fabric. This early development triggered additional strategic development throughout the decade, and Sundance Square now contains numerous residential units, movie theaters, restaurants, and shops; 6,000 new parking spaces; and over 500,000 square feet (46,500 m²) of office space. In addition to the project's commercial success, Sundance Square has greatly bolstered downtown's civic and cultural infrastructure through numerous projects, including the Fort Worth Central Library, the Nancy Lee and Perry R. Bass Performance Hall, and the Maddox-Muse Center. Sundance Square's management operates with a focus on security, parking, and cleanliness, the three amenities deemed most critical for residents and visitors.

Although the master plan is largely complete, Sundance Square continues to add new space and uses to the market, and it continues to set new standards. In 2008, Sundance Square began purchasing cleaner, renewable energy to offset 10 percent of its yearly energy needs for the next five years. According to the Environmental Protection Agency, Sundance Square is the largest green power purchaser in Texas among the agency's real estate partners and the second-largest nationally within the real estate industry. Sundance Square also enjoys high occupancy and rental rates that outperform the Dallas–Fort Worth market. The thoughtful vision laid out more than 25 years ago continues to pay dividends today and has facilitated the rebirth of downtown Fort Worth as a viable, pedestrian-rich, and dynamic urban center.

PROJECT DATA

Web Site
www.sundancesquaremanagement.
  com

Site Area
38 city blocks (59 ac/23.8 ha)

Facilities
509,395 sf (47,324 m²) office
120,963 sf (11,238 m²) retail
118 multifamily units
213 parking spaces

Land Use
office, retail, restaurant,
  entertainment, residential, parking
  garage, civic

Start/Completion Dates
June 1988–December 2009

55

RESIDENT

AL

Madison at 14th Apartments

OAKLAND, CALIFORNIA

Madison at 14th Apartments effectively mitigates the deleterious effects of two holes in downtown Oakland, one physical and the other social. Built on a former surface parking lot, this eight-story infill mid-rise introduces a striking, contemporary design to the area while plugging a jarring gap in the urban fabric. On a deeper level, this 79-unit apartment building with street-level shops and restaurants addresses the need for affordable housing and designates housing opportunities and services for former foster care youth. With Madison at 14th Apartments, Affordable Housing Associates (AHA), in partnership with First Place for Youth (FPFY), has achieved something laudable and worthy of emulation.

JURY STATEMENT

Madison at 14th Apartments combines award-winning contemporary architecture with a social mission. Twenty of the 79 units are reserved for former foster youths, thousands of whom emerge from California's foster care system each year with no family support or social safety net. In addition to housing opportunities, the former foster youths are offered job training, education, and life-skills programs.

DEVELOPMENT TEAM

Owner/Developer
Affordable Housing Associates
Berkeley, California
www.ahainc.org

Transitional Services Provider
First Place for Youth
Oakland, California
www.firstplaceforyouth.com

Architect
Leddy Maytum Stacy Architects
San Francisco, California
www.lmsarch.com

Architecturally, the building respects downtown's rich architectural heritage while achieving exceptional design and functionality within a limited footprint. The development achieves a density rate of 241 dwelling units per acre without sacrificing unit quality. The 79 apartment units have large windows and are constructed from sustainable materials to promote healthy, ecological living. A 27-kilowatt rooftop photovoltaic system provides 30 to 50 percent of the building's electrical common load, and a hydronic heating system offers an alternative to forced-air or electric heat. A three-tiered parking-lift system, powered by vegetable oil, accommodates 53 cars in a space that could fit only 17 without the lift. At the base of the building, 2,600 square feet (240 m²) of fully leased retail and restaurant space brings life to the streetscape.

Although the design of the building by Leddy Maytum Stacy Architects merits attention, the programmatic mission of the building is truly impressive. AHA has set aside 59 units for people earning

PHOTOGRAPHS BY TIM GRIFFITH (ALL IMAGES)

30 to 60 percent of the area median income, and the remaining 20 units are reserved for youth recently emancipated from the foster care system. FPFY approached AHA with some powerful statistics regarding foster youth that led AHA to partner with FPFY. Every year, hundreds of foster youth are emancipated from Oakland's foster care system, but most have no support network. Consequently, 40 percent become homeless within a few months. The 20 former foster youth who live in Madison at 14th participate in a two-year First Steps program facilitated by FPFY. In this program, they learn valuable life skills and pay an increasing portion of their rent as they become economically self-sufficient. Thus far, the program has produced tremendous results. All 20 youth have retained their housing, half are pursuing postsecondary education, and 42 percent are employed.

The response to Madison at 14th has been overwhelming at all levels. More than 3,000 households applied to live in the complex, and the building has enjoyed a constant occupancy rate of 100 percent. The American Institute of Architects bestowed its National Housing Award in 2009 to Madison at 14th Apartments. The attention and accolades from all places reveal a strong demand for this type of development. Cities everywhere are grappling with serious physical and social challenges, and Madison at 14th Apartments offers a compelling example of how to address both.

PROJECT DATA

Web Site
www.ahainc.org

Site Area
0.33 ac (0.13 ha)

Facilities
2,000 sf (186 m²) office
2,800 sf (260 m²) retail
79 multifamily units
53 parking spaces

Land Use
residential, retail, restaurant, garage
  parking, open space, educational/
  social services

Start/Completion Dates
August 2006–April 2008

Newton Suites

SINGAPORE

Newton Suites is a 118-unit residential building designed to show that environmentally sustainable design and high-rise luxury are compatible. The 36-story apartment tower's exterior uses sunshading elements, protruding balconies, and expansive windows to manage the sun's light and energy potential, while vertical green walls and communal gardens bring lush greenery to the skies. The S$23.5 million project uses passive cooling techniques to combine outdoor and indoor living space in a high-rise building, offering a model for other tropical cities.

Rising 121 meters (397 ft), Newton Suites sits at the edge of a high-rise zone and fronts a height-controlled area, affording expansive views of Singapore's central nature reserves—a rare luxury in the densely built city-state. The building is raised off the ground, mitigating noise pollution from the streets and affording even the lowest-level units expansive views. The 0.39-hectare (0.95-ac) site is located in Novena, a district that features only privately owned housing—an anomaly in Singapore, where 80 to 90 percent of the population lives in housing provided by the city-state's Housing and Development Board. The high-rise tower is located near a rapid-transit station and a large shopping mall.

JURY STATEMENT

An environmentally sensitive residential tower, 118-unit Newton Suites uses a number of green design techniques including sun shading, rooftop plantings, cross ventilation, and a vertical green wall that climbs the height of the building.

DEVELOPMENT TEAM

Owner/Developer
UOL Group Limited
Singapore
www.uol.com.sg

Design Architect
WOHA Architects Pte Ltd.
Singapore
www.woha-architects.com

PHOTOGRAPHS BY PATRICK BINGHAM HALL (62, 65);
ALBERT LIM (63L, 63R); TIM GRIFFITH (64L, 64R)

Designed by WOHA Architects, the 118 residential units are stacked four residences per floor, with balconies oriented toward the nature reserve or city center. The two- and three-bedroom apartments share communal sky gardens that cantilever over the southeastern facade on every fourth floor. These protruding gardens and balconies offer outdoor living spaces in the air, and together with sunshading screens they shelter the units from the sun. Along with ample cross ventilation, this shade helps keep the units livable in Singapore's tropical climate. The angled, mesh sunshades also create an expressive facade, which changes appearance depending on the angle of the sun and the observer's vantage point.

Landscaping is a prominent element at Newton Suites: rooftop plantings, lush sky gardens, and green walls are central to the design. Most available horizontal and vertical surfaces are landscaped: trees cover the parking garage, project from the sky gardens at every four levels, and crown the building at the penthouse roof decks. A high-rise tangle of trumpet vine climbs more than 100 meters (328 ft) up the side of the residential tower. The incorporation of nature into the design highlights the importance of green space and sustainability without sacrificing comfort, artistic vision, or urban density.

The recreation deck, which includes a terrace for socializing, a sauna, a steam room, a gymnasium complex, and a swimming pool, is built on the roof of the above-ground parking garage. Vine-covered screen enclosures reduce negative byproducts from the cars and reduce energy requirements. The roof and walls of the gymnasium match the checkered arrangement of painted panels that covers the planar surfaces of the residential tower, thus uniting the two buildings and providing a hard-edged counterpoint to the softness of the surrounding water and vegetation.

The residences are offered as freehold properties—meaning the buyer owns the property in perpetuity, unlike leaseholds, where ownership expires after a set term—which is a desirable arrangement in Singapore. All 118 units were sold within a year of the sales launch. The developer targeted young professionals and those looking to move from public housing to privately owned residences. The project has won several awards, including the Emporis Skyscraper Award's Silver Medal in 2007 and a special commendation for the 2008 International Highrise Award.

PROJECT DATA

Web Site
www.uol.com.sg/corporate/our_
    business/residential/completed_
    projects/newton_suites.html

Site Area
0.39 ha (0.95 ac)

Facilities
118 multifamily units
125 parking spaces

Land Uses
residential, parking

Start/Completion Dates
December 2003–September 2007

Palazzo Tornabuoni

FLORENCE, ITALY

The meticulous adaptive use and restoration of Florence's 15th-century Palazzo Tornabuoni as an opulent mix of 38 residences, boutique retail, and restaurant space has elevated an entire section of this cultured city. Occupying a full city block and home to numerous artistic treasures from the 15th through the 17th centuries, Palazzo Tornabuoni possesses an architectural splendor on par with some of Florence's finest edifices. Kitewood Partners and R.D.M. Real Estate Development spared no expense in this premier project. Their investment in Palazzo Tornabuoni has enriched the city's urban fabric while offering the first private residence club in Italy—and one of the

JURY STATEMENT

Palazzo Tornabuoni, a 17,000-square-meter mixed-use project that encompasses a full city block in Florence, features a high-end fractional ownership development, luxury retailers, offices, and restaurants. The project includes a meticulous restoration of a 15th-century palazzo and its museum-quality frescos, micro-mosaics, and statues, maintaining strong links to the historic fabric of Florence while offering many new features and amenities.

DEVELOPMENT TEAM

Developers
Kitebrook Partners
Washington, D.C.
www.kitebrook.com

R.D.M. Real Estate Development
Florence, Italy

Design Architect
G & B s.r.l.
Florence, Italy
www.gebstudio.com

PHOTOGRAPHS BY ROBERTO QUAGLI (66); LEO
BIEBER (67L); FRANCESCO BEDINI (67R, 69R); JAMES
O'MARA (68); MASSIMO LISTRI (69L)

finest in Europe. One EMEA juror described the project as "a historic restoration of exceptional quality to create a masterpiece in the center of Florence."

Constructed for Giovanni Tornabuoni in the 15th century, the palace has enjoyed a storied history. The powerful Medici family owned it during the Renaissance, and Pope Leo XI dwelt there as well. According to music scholars, the world's first opera was written and performed in the palace. Although the palace enjoyed a long succession of wealthy owners who patronized the arts, it lost some of its luster over the last couple centuries. For the past 100 years, the 17,000-square-meter (183,000-sf) palace served as a bank headquarters.

The exacting restoration of the palace to its original glory took four years under the supervision of Florence's Soprintendenza ai Beni Artistici e Storici, or superintendent of fine arts and history. The renovation included not only the building but also every single piece of museum-quality artwork. Internationally renowned architect Michele Bonan designed the interior space and achieved a balance between the building's historic grand and contemporary flair for the new residential units.

Marketed as the Palace Residence Club, Palazzo Tornabuoni offers 38 residential units. Owners may purchase membership in a studio, one-bedroom, or two-bedroom unit, and a handful of residences are available for full ownership. The initial sales release of 20 units included eight memberships for each residence. Prices started at €218,000, €364,000, and €549,000 for studios, one bedrooms, and two bedrooms, respectively. The limited number of full-ownership units range from €1.2 million to €6 million. Four Seasons Hotels and Resorts currently manages the private residence club and provides a host of amenities to members. The retail space is 100 percent occupied and features two restaurants, one highlighted by Michelin as Florence's best, as well as luxury retailers such as Cartier, Bulgari, Bottega Veneta, and Max Mara. In addition to complementing the streetscape with its renewed splendor, Palazzo Tornabuoni complements Florence's broader effort to move away from quick, one-stop tourism toward high-quality, "stay awhile" tourism. With the magnificence available at Palazzo Tornabuoni, discerning consumers can have a home away from home in the heart of Tuscany.

PROJECT DATA

Web Site
www.palazzotornabuoni.com

Site Area
0.4 ha (0.98 ac)

Facilities
4,100 m² (44,100 sf) retail/
   restaurant/entertainment
38 residential units

Land Use
residential, retail, restaurant

Start/Completion Dates
2005–2010

The Visionaire

NEW YORK, NEW YORK

The Visionaire in Battery Park City, Lower Manhattan, is the Albanese Organization's latest and most advanced residential building, a 35-story, 537,400-square-foot (49,900-m²) condominium tower. Designed by Pelli Clarke Pelli Architects, the $310 million glass and terra-cotta tower features a unique, curved facade and comprises 246 condominium units, 4,300 square feet (400 m²) of retail space designated for an organic and local food market, and a 44,000-square-foot (4,090-m²) maintenance facility for the Battery Park City Parks Conservancy. The LEED-Platinum building is designed to yield 35 percent more energy savings than traditional code-compliant buildings.

The Albanese Organization, a full-service real estate firm based in New York, has built three green luxury residential buildings in Battery Park City since 2003. Each building's design evolved from its pre-

DEVELOPMENT TEAM

Owner/Developer
Albanese Organization, Inc.
Garden City, New York
www.albaneseorg.com

Co-Venture Partner
Starwood Capital Group
Greenwich, Connecticut
www.starwoodcapital.com

Design Architect
Pelli Clarke Pelli Architects
New York, New York
www.pcparch.com

JURY STATEMENT

The 35-story Visionaire—combining 246 residences, an organic and local food market, and a 44,000-square-foot maintenance facility—has obtained LEED-Platinum certification through enhanced indoor air quality, geothermal wells, photovoltaic solar panels, an on-site blackwater treatment plant, and a natural gas–fired microturbine, reducing potable water use by 29 percent and aggregate energy use by 42 percent.

decessor, adopting new technologies and taking advantage of the emerging market for green buildings. Solaire was North America's first green residential high rise; Verdesian became the nation's first LEED-Platinum residential high rise; and the Visionaire has won numerous awards for its sustainability.

The Visionaire is sited on the last remaining multifamily parcel in Battery Park City, which was formerly a surface parking lot. Architect Rafael Pelli designed a tower with a curved facade, torqued to maximize natural light and provide views of either Manhattan or New York Harbor from all four sides of the building. The structure's base conforms to the stringent Battery Park City design guidelines, which require the project to fit seamlessly into the urban context and street grid at ground level. The guidelines call for red brick; in response, Pelli used a terra-cotta-colored panel and glass curtain wall that visually blends with the brick of surrounding buildings without using the prescribed material.

The Visionaire's sustainable strategies go well beyond bike racks and hybrid-car parking spaces to renewable energy generation and innovative water conservation strategies. The building uses a 25,000-gallon (94,600-L) bioreactor to treat blackwater—wastewater from kitchens and bathrooms—recycling it as toilet water or cooling fluid for the air-conditioning system. The landscaped roof gardens reduce the heat-island effect and funnel stormwater into a 10,000-gallon (37,900-L) rainwater storage tank that provides water for irrigation. The Albanese Organization estimates that the wastewater treatment system saves the building 25,000 gallons (94,600 L) of potable water per day, and the rainwater catchment system can harvest up to 12,000 gallons (45,400 L) at one time.

A gas-fired microturbine produces 20 percent of energy needs; a waste-heat recovery system heats hot water; geothermal systems heat and cool the Battery Park City Conservancy's offices; and 35 per-

PHOTOGRAPHS BY JEFF GOLDBERG, ESTO
PHOTOGRAPHY (70, 71L, 71R, 73); PCP ARCHITECTS (72)

cent of the building's electric energy is supplied through wind-generated power. Energy modeling established the optimal configuration of the 48-kilowatt photovoltaic system, and a highly efficient curtain wall contributes to greater insulation. Elevators use a regenerative motor—capturing and reusing energy from braking— that reduces electricity consumption by 30 percent. Also, all of the heating, cooling, and lighting systems are tied to a central building management system, which is monitored round the clock by the concierge and building manager.

High-quality water and air systems were also central tenets of the Albanese Organization's sustainable design. "Tenants always tell us how much their life and their health have improved since they moved into our green buildings here," Chris Albanese, partner at the Albanese Organization, says. "That's what's most satisfying for us." The Visionaire's internal high-efficiency air filtration system continually replenishes and cleanses the air, filtering it twice before returning it to the units. A centralized water filtration system provides purified water to the baths, showers, faucets, and ice makers in all residences. The Albanese Organization hopes these efforts will foster good health in homeowners as well as reduce or eliminate the need for residents to purchase bottled water.

The Albanese Organization's eight-year odyssey of green building in Battery Park City has paid off with the Visionaire, the developer's most sustainable building to date. According to Albanese, "Through an integrated design approach, the Visionaire maximizes energy efficiency while minimizing impact on the external environment," resulting in a reduction of potable water usage by 29 percent and aggregate energy use by 42 percent.

PROJECT DATA

Web Site
www.thevisionaire.com

Site Area
0.67 ac (0.27 ha)

Facilities
44,000 sf (4,090 m²) office
4,300 sf (400 m²) retail
246 multifamily units
110 parking spaces

Land Use
residential, office, retail, civic

Start/Completion Dates
August 2006–April 2009

CIVI

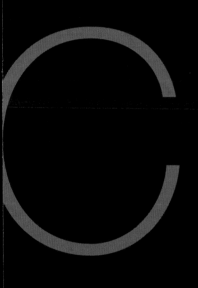

Battery Park City Master Plan

NEW YORK, NEW YORK

DEVELOPMENT TEAM

Owner/Developer/Master Planner
Battery Park City Authority
New York, New York
www.batteryparkcity.org

The Battery Park City Master Plan, adopted in 1979, has facilitated the private development of 8 million square feet (743,000 m²) of commercial space, 7.2 million square feet (669,000 m²) of residential space, and nearly 36 acres (14 ha) of open space in lower Manhattan, becoming a model for successful large-scale planning efforts. The strength of the master plan has allowed development to occur incrementally, thereby creating a neighborhood with a stable mix of uses and diverse architecture that blends into the existing New York City street grid. "The Battery Park City

JURY STATEMENT

Representing a positive shift from the urban renewal mindset of the 1960s and 1970s, the Battery Park City Master Plan has facilitated the private development of 8 million square feet of commercial space, 7.2 million square feet of residential space, and nearly 36 acres of open space in lower Manhattan, becoming an international model for public/private partnerships on a grand scale.

Master Plan represents a positive shift away from the urban renewal mindset of the 1960s and 1970s. The plan has been responsive to changing conditions—such as the emergence of energy-efficient buildings—but has remained true to its original intent," according to Joe Brown, chief executive, planning, design, and development at AECOM and chairman of the ULI Global Awards for Excellence.

The original master plan for Battery Park City was developed during the 1960s under New York governor Nelson Rockefeller. Early ideas for the "city within a city" envisioned the area as a continuous 100-acre (40.5-ha) truck dock and warehouse to bring shipping companies back to Manhattan. However, this plan was quickly scrapped, and a new team of planners and designers sketched out a community reminiscent of a 1960s beach resort—hoping to offer homeowners an oasis in lower Manhattan and office tenants an alternate destination to the buzzing financial district. This design was meant to exemplify an innovative "city of the future" with a protected pedestrian realm, urban open space, and integrated transportation options. In 1962, however, the idea of combining housing, offices, and light industry was not well received.

Governor Rockefeller hired architect Wallace K. Harrison to design the second generation of the plan. Harrison was tasked with inventing a model community that was the antithesis of the slums plaguing New York City at the time. The result was a socially diverse, mixed-income community: the plan sought to create safe streets, ample parks and green spaces, and healthy buildings where every unit received abundant sunshine and fresh air. Harrison's proposal relied heavily on strong social programs and, coinciding with dwindling approval of the city's public housing policies, met with vehement public resistance.

In 1969, a collaborative city/state design team created the final master plan. Although well received by all of the stakeholders, the plan was held up by the 1973 recession, stagnating until a financial emergency in 1979 caused New York State's Urban Development Corporation to condemn the project and transfer the title from the city to the Battery Park City Authority. The authority acted quickly to devise and adopt a new master plan. The goals of this plan were simple: expand lower Manhattan, encourage people to live downtown, and increase the amount of green space and trees in the region. The new plan extended the city's existing street grid in blocks that could be parceled out to different developers as the market allowed.

The September 11, 2001, terrorist attacks had a major impact on Battery Park City. Many residents were displaced because of toxic dust and smoke, the immediately affected area was closed off and declared a crime scene, and a number of residential buildings were seriously damaged. Since the attacks, however, the neighborhood has been resurgent, with more than a dozen new buildings—including the Goldman Sachs Group World Headquarters, the Visionaire, and Riverhouse.

Even though it has been continually reinvented, all iterations of the master plan were based on four core values: productive public/private partnerships, balance and aesthetics, environmental responsibility, and public benefit. Today, with its rich mix of residential and commercial uses, the area is home to 9,000 residents, 52 shops and service providers, 22 restaurants, a movie theater, two hotels, almost 36 acres (14 ha) of parks, 20 works of public art, three public schools, a marina, a 1.2-mile (1.9-km) esplanade, the Irish Hunger Memorial, the Museum of Jewish Heritage, the New York Police Memorial, and the Skyscraper Museum.

PROJECT DATA

Web Site
www.batteryparkcity.org

Site Area
92 ac (37.2 ha)

Facilities
8 million sf (743,000 m²) current (9.8 million sf [910,500 m²] at buildout) commercial
8,000 multifamily units (8,500 at buildout)
765 hotel rooms
1,300 parking spaces

Land Use
office, residential, retail, hotel, restaurant, education, museums, marina, open space, parking

Start/Completion Dates
November 1969–2010 (projected)

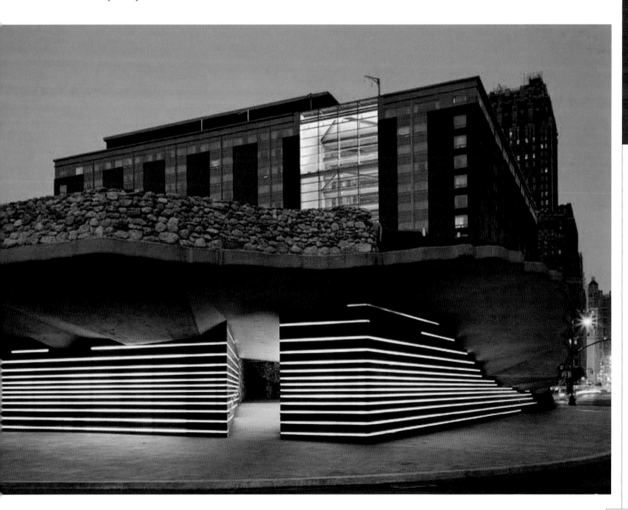

ULI Amanda Burden
urban open space
Award

Campus Martius Park

DETROIT, MICHIGAN

Detroiters and national observers alike have raved about Campus Martius since it opened in November 2004 at the city's historic crossroads, a once gritty intersection where five major streets converge. The inaugural winner of the Amanda Burden Urban Open Space Award, the project is a 2.5-acre (1-ha) oasis of imaginative horticulture, green granite walls, and crushed limestone paths, returning vibrancy and spurring investment in the formerly downtrodden downtown. The $20 million urban park manages to serve as both a peaceful refuge and a popular destination that attracts more than 2 million visitors a year.

JURY STATEMENT

Known as "Detroit's Official Gathering Place," Campus Martius Park is a vibrant central square that has become the heart of the city's downtown redevelopment initiative. With extensive landscaping, movable seating, and an ice-skating rink, it serves as a much-needed recreational respite and an entertainment venue that is breathing new life into the area.

DEVELOPMENT TEAM

Owner/Developer
Detroit 300 Conservancy
Detroit, Michigan
www.campusmartiuspark.org

Design Architect
Rundell Ernstberger Associates, LLC
Indianapolis, Indiana
www.reasite.com

The neighborhood around the park has been the center of town for centuries. In 1805, when Detroit—already 104 years old—began rebuilding after a fire destroyed the frontier community, leaders plotted the future metropolis from the so-called Point of Origin on land known as the Campus Martius, Latin for "the Field of Mars." Detroit grew into the industrial powerhouse that was the nation's fourth-most-populous city from the 1920s to the 1940s and still fifth largest in the 1950s and 1960s. But jobs and residents began leaving as suburbanization took hold and the automobile industry's presence in the city began to shrink. The population has been halved in 60 years, and the number of downtown jobs fell from more than 150,000 in the 1960s to 60,000 in the 1990s. A survey in 1996 found 80 percent of the 67 buildings in the city center were empty, accounting for 6 million square feet (560,000 m²) of space.

To stem this massive disinvestment, a group of businesspeople and civic leaders joined in the Detroit 300 Conservancy and eventually decided to develop Campus Martius Park as a legacy gift to the city of Detroit. Led by Edsel B. Ford II, a businessman and the great-grandson of Henry Ford, Detroit 300 raised $20 million toward the park's construction.

PHOTOGRAPHS BY DETROIT 300 CONSERVANCY (80, 81, 83); ARA HOWRANI (82)

Designed by Indianapolis-based Rundell Ernstberger Associates, the park serves as "Detroit's Official Gathering Place." Water runs along wavy granite walls that border the west side of the park, and in the southeast corner, surrounding an elaborate 1872 Civil War monument, is a smaller waterworks. The Point of Origin, a survey marker from which the coordinate system of Detroit was planned, is marked by a medallion laid in granite and covered by a glass portal at the center of a compass emblazoned in concrete pavers. Trees shelter the park, and two lush lawns divided by the central fountain are sunk slightly below street level, giving visitors a sense of protection from the passing traffic.

Just like the movable chairs that allow park visitors to arrange their own seating, the park transforms itself on a bigger scale: stages rise from the ground at both ends of the north lawn, and with specially designed lighting and sound, the park becomes an open-air theater for concerts, films, and other events. When the weather starts turning cold in the fall, workers assemble the popular skating rink for winter; a plinth above the idle fountain serves as a setting for a large Christmas tree or other movable focal elements.

Of no small benefit to the struggling city, Campus Martius has delivered a positive economic effect. Two major office buildings have risen adjacent to the site, and residential developments and restaurants have opened nearby. The Compuware Corporation, Quicken Loans, and GalaxE.Solutions have relocated to buildings adjacent to the park, bringing more than 6,000 workers downtown. Experts estimate $500 million of investment has flowed into the area since plans for the park were announced.

PROJECT DATA

Web Site
www.campusmartiuspark.org

Site Area
2.5 ac (1.0 ha)

Land Use
open space, restaurant

Start/Completion Dates
May 2003–November 2004

Dragon Lake Bridge Park

BENGBU, ANHUI PROVINCE, CHINA

Beijing and Shanghai enjoy tremendous attention for their bold new development, but many of China's often overlooked second-tier cities are engaging in endeavors that are just as intrepid. Dragon Lake Bridge Park in the city of Bengbu, located in Anhui Province, provides a powerful example of how landscape design can transform a city's identity as well as the way people connect with one another and with nature. AECOM's design of the $40 million, 25-hectare (62-ac)

JURY STATEMENT

The 25-hectare Dragon Lake Bridge Park, in the second-tier city of Bengbu, restores a heavily polluted lake, returning it to recreational use and raising the values of the surrounding land.

DEVELOPMENT TEAM

Owner/Developer
Xincheng Comprehensive
  Development Zone Bengbu
Bengbu, Anhui, China

Master Planner/Design Architect
AECOM
Los Angeles, California
www.aecom.com

PHOTOGRAPHS BY DIXI CARRILLO (ALL PHOTOS)

PROJECT DATA

Web Site
www.aecom.com/What+We+Do/
Design+and+Planning/stories/
In+China

Site Area
25 ha (71.6 ac)

Facilities
2,000 m² (21,500 sf) retail/
restaurant/entertainment

Land Use
park, retail, restaurant, entertainment,
education, marina, surface parking

Start/Completion Dates
May 2005–May 2009

park succeeds in enhancing the environment and quality of life for the city as a whole, in promoting tourism and investment, and in creating a contemporary space that celebrates local culture while strengthening public awareness of the natural and built environments.

Bengbu, which means "clam wharf" in Chinese, has a heritage closely associated with the water because of its proximity to the Huai River and Dragon Lake. A former center of the freshwater pearl industry, the city has seen rapid urbanization and industrial development and is now a major hub for food processing. Bengbu has grown east from the banks of the river and will eventually encompass Dragon Lake. Although growth has brought a certain level of prosperity, it has exacted a high environmental toll. Dragon Lake, once replete with fishing and recreational activities, had become eutrophic. Its water quality had deteriorated to the point where human contact was ill-advised. To mitigate these deleterious effects and reposition Dragon Lake as a focal point for the region, the city hired AECOM and initiated a master-planning process for the Dragon Lake Scenic Area in 2004.

The master plan identified three major objectives: first, the improvement of water quality as a key landscape design aim; second, the enrichment of cultural and recreational offerings available to the larger community; and last, the establishment of a new lake district and a signature lakeside park at the western shore to provide a meaningful interface between the city and the lake. Critical to the plan's success was the involvement of the public. AECOM and the city conducted many interviews and revealed the design for the park at the very early stages to solicit feedback.

The first steps in creating Dragon Lake Bridge Park revolved around improving the lake's water quality and stabilizing the ecosystem. AECOM used a variety of measures and technologies, such as artificial circulation and aeration, construction of wetlands, and restoration of vegetated riparian buffers.

The design team altered the topography to create a terraced landscape that allows a continuous flow of visitors along the lakefront. A massive greenbelt of indigenous trees and plants anchor the site to its natural setting. This focus on localism and ecological sensitivity has created new natural habitats while minimizing irrigation and maintenance costs. In addition to the park's extensive landscape design and habitat restoration, the park offers cultural spaces and elements that instill a distinctive, contemporary Chinese character to the landscape. The Bamboo Garden and Celebration Plaza anchor the core of the park, and outdoor sculpture as well as exhibition and gallery space abound amid the walkways, pavilions, bridges, and terraces.

As Bengbu moves into the future, it does so as a progressive lakeside city. Dragon Lake Bridge Park has become a signature amenity that showcases the city's potential while offering residents and visitors a significant asset. Juror S. C. Liu, chairman of MyTopHome, commented how "Dragon Bridge Park is exemplary in terms of environmental and investment considerations ... [and is] evidence of how a well-planned project can bring multifaceted advantages to a city and its people."

MUMUTH

GRAZ, AUSTRIA

The Haus für Musik and Musiktheater (MUMUTH; House of Music and Music Drama) is a multipurpose theater in the cultural center of Graz, Austria. Designed by the Amsterdam-based UNStudio, the gently bulging four-story structure is shrouded by a thin stainless-steel mesh and organized around a load-bearing spiral staircase. Developed by state-owned Bundesimmobiliengesellschaft and opened in March 2009, the 6,200-square-meter (67,000-sf) project features a 450-seat theater alongside a restaurant, rehearsal rooms, and workshops for 2,100 students.

JURY STATEMENT

MUMUTH Music Theatre, part of the University of Music and Performing Arts in Graz, is a 6,167-square-meter performance art facility within the city's cultural center. The design, based on a "blob-to-box" model—the "blob" giving shape to the public spaces, the "box" forming the multiuse performance hall—is connected by a central spiral staircase that creates column-free space among the theater, high-tech acoustic laboratory, and restaurant areas.

DEVELOPMENT TEAM

Owner/Developer
Bundesimmobiliengesellschaft (BIG)
Vienna, Austria
www.big.at

Design Architect
UNStudio
Amsterdam, the Netherlands
www.unstudio.com/nl

MUMUTH was the result of a design competition held by Kunstuniversität Graz, the University of Music and Performing Arts of Graz, more than a decade ago. Based on the relationship between music and design, UNStudio's design was selected over 212 other entrants. Various forces—the city's reluctance to detract attention from other sponsored projects and ongoing funding issues— conspired to delay the project. Only after the 2005 elections was funding returned, allowing UNStudio's design to become a reality.

Graz, the second-largest city in Austria, is home to the largest population of university students in the country. It also has a storied architectural history: its Old Town is considered one of the best-preserved city centers in central Europe. Its status presented a challenge to the designers of MUMUTH: integrate a modern structure into the neoclassical backdrop of Graz's Lichtenfelsgasse Street. UNStudio elected not to assimilate the building architecturally but instead to focus on the nexus of music and design, creating a place where both the city's students and patrons of music could come together.

UNStudio's design is based on a "blob-to-box" model: the "blob" gives shape to the public spaces, with the "box" forming the multiuse performance hall. The two design concepts are connected by a central spiral staircase that creates column-free space, freeing the spacious floor plans for other uses and opening up sight lines throughout. The designers conceptualized this staircase as a spring

PHOTOGRAPHS BY IWAN BAAN (88, 90, 91L, 91R);
ROB HOEKSTRA (89L); CHRISTIAN RICHTERS (89R)

that stretches through each of the four floors, giving form to and carrying the load of the three floors above. This spiral, which repeats itself, recalls the dynamics of musical scales, creating a parallel between the building's form and function. The staircase is a composite of steel and concrete, its form so precise that it required the use of self-compacting concrete pumped from below rather than the traditional method of pouring from above.

Intended for both educational and performance uses, the building is multifunctional, incorporating different programs and logistics in one building. For example, custom-designed acoustic panels are adjustable to meet the sound requirements of varying performance types. Also, the performance hall's 108 floor modules can rise hydraulically, creating different room and stage configurations—necessary technologies for a hall expected to be reconfigured at least three times a week.

The facade also embodies the building's versatility: the stainless-steel mesh appears opaque in the daylight, when the building is open only to students; however, at night the mesh appears transparent, illuminated from inside for theatrical performances open to the public. Two entrances also demarcate the building's functions: during the day, students enter from the adjacent park; at night, patrons are welcomed through the street entrance. The facade's purpose is not just aesthetic; it helps reduce the project's heat load by approximately 50 percent. From the flexible performance spaces to the technologically advanced architecture and acoustics, MUMUTH has become one of the most advanced and dynamic performance spaces in Europe.

PROJECT DATA

Web Site
www.unstudio.com/nl/unstudio/
projects/music-theatre

Site Area
0.27 hectare (0.68 ac)

Facilities
162 m² (1,744 sf) office
1,870 m² (20,129 sf) retail/
entertainment

Land Uses
restaurant, office, entertainment,
education

Start/Completion Dates
March 2006–March 2009

PHOTOGRAPHS BY

Vancouver Convention Centre West

VANCOUVER, BRITISH COLUMBIA, CANADA

Vancouver Convention Centre West eschews the traditional model of convention center design, opting instead to blend into both the built and the natural environments in downtown Vancouver. Simultaneously a building, an urban destination, a park, and an ecosystem, the 111,500-square-meter (1.2 million-sf) convention center sits low on the waterfront,

DEVELOPMENT TEAM

Owner/Developer
BC Pavilion Corporation
Vancouver, British Columbia, Canada
www.bcpavco.com

Design Architect
LMN Architects
Seattle, Washington
www.lmnarchitects.com

JURY STATEMENT

Knit into the urban fabric of Vancouver's downtown core, the 1.2 million-square-foot Vancouver Convention Centre West establishes an important link to the city's park system, connecting the existing harbor greenbelt with a major civic plaza and a six-acre living roof—one of the largest in Canada.

PHOTOGRAPHS BY LMN ARCHITECTS (92); NIC
LEHOUX PHOTOGRAPHY (93, 94L, 94R); LMN/STUDIO
216 (95)

preserving existing vistas from downtown. Occupying a former brownfield site, the C$883 million Vancouver Convention Centre West features 92,900 square meters (1 million sf) of convention space, 8,400 square meters (90,000 sf) of retail space, and 37,200 meters (400,000 sf) of walkways, bikeways, public open space, and plazas. The LEED-Platinum public building is capped by a 2.4-hectare (6-ac) living roof—one of the largest in Canada.

The central design challenge faced by Seattle-based LMN Architects was to integrate the convention center at the intersection of the urban realm and the marine habitat. Situated on an 8.9-hectare (22-ac) site—5.7 hectares (14 ac) on land, 3.2 hectares (8 ac) built over water—the building's low-slung form is a result of city ordinances requiring the preservation of view corridors from the downtown core onto Vancouver Harbour. The building's folded form not only responded to these corridors, modulating to extend the lines of adjacent downtown streets, but also was a design consideration, mirroring the topography of the region and creating a connection to the North Shore mountains seen across the Burrard Inlet.

The most visible evidence of the project's thoughtful approach to ecological design is its living roof—the building's "fifth elevation"—which hosts more than 400,000 indigenous plants and a colony of 60,000 bees. Biologically, the green roof is the terminus of a chain of waterfront parks that ring the harbor and create a continuous habitat between the convention center and Vancouver's Stanley Park. Along the perimeter facing the water, an artificial reef built of concrete drops below the public walkway along the waterfront. The reef is designed in collaboration with marine biologists to function as part of the natural shoreline, supporting salmon, crabs, and a variety of other native marine species.

Vancouver Convention Centre West uses a host of sustainable strategies to reduce its ecological footprint. A seawater heat pump system, for example, takes advantage of the constant temperature of seawater to produce cooling for the building during warmer months and heating in the cooler months. A blackwater treatment plant and desalinization plant are situated on site. Along with a gray-water recycling system, this water conservation strategy reduces potable water use by 60 to 70 percent over typical convention centers.

Planning took place over three years, with dozens of meetings and presentations involving city officials, residents, and local businesses. The environmental impact of the waterfront development was extensively reviewed, requiring multiple meetings with the Department of Fisheries for marine habitat design and project mitigation as well as the convening of a 40-person sustainability committee to address the green building strategies. The extensive involvement of the community in the design process was made manifest in the accessible nature of the convention center, which includes continuous public access to the water's edge through walkways, bikeways, public open space, and plazas. Through extensive public collaboration and sustainable design, Vancouver Convention Centre West successfully blends the complex ecology, vibrant local culture, and dense urban environment of downtown Vancouver.

PROJECT DATA

Web Site
www.vancouverconventioncentre.
 com

Site Area
11.1 ha (27.5 ac)

Facilities
20,700 m² (223,000 sf) exhibition
 space
10,700 m² (115,000 sf) meeting space
8,800 m² (95,000 sf) retail

Land Use
exhibition space, office, retail,
 entertainment, restaurants,
 open space

Start/Completion Dates
2003–April 2009

The Americas Jury

Marty Jones, Jury Chair
Boston, Massachusetts

Marty Jones is president of Corcoran Jennison Company, a Boston-based, full-service real estate organization. Jones began her career in housing with the U.S. Department of Housing and Urban Development. Since joining Corcoran Jennison in 1979, she has been responsible for developing and financing the company's mixed-income, affordable housing and urban revitalization projects, and for asset management of the company's multifamily housing portfolio.

A graduate of Brown University, where she received a degree in urban studies, Jones has served as a trustee of the Urban Land Institute and was a founding member of New England Women in Real Estate. She has been recognized for her work in the redevelopment of public housing projects and in building community partnerships with low-income resident associations.

Michael Balaban
Washington, D.C.

Michael Balaban is president of Lowe Enterprises Real Estate Group, Eastern Region, with overall responsibility for commercial property investment, development, and management activities in the region. Previously, Balaban was the acquisitions officer of the Washington Real Estate Investment Trust. Prior to that, he was a Massachusetts-registered architect and real estate consultant active in the New England area.

Balaban received a bachelor's degree from Kenyon College, a master's in architecture from Harvard Graduate School of Design, and a master's of business administration from the University of Pennsylvania.

Amanda Burden
New York, New York

Amanda Burden is chair of the New York City Planning Commission and director of the New York Department of City Planning. Her commitment to making the public realm a focal point of land use planning is apparent throughout New York, including such notable projects as the High Line, an abandoned elevated rail line in Manhattan that the city has started transforming into a unique elevated linear park. More than 30 projects, many by world-renowned architects, have been catalyzed by the plan.

Burden received a BA at Sarah Lawrence College and an MS in urban planning at Columbia University Graduate School of Architecture. In 2009, she was chosen as the winner of the Urban Land Institute's J.C. Nichols Prize for Visionaries in Urban Development, its highest honor for an individual. The prize comes with a $100,000 honorarium, which Burden donated to ULI to create an annual prize to honor transformative and exciting public urban open spaces.

Thomas Cody
Portland, Oregon

Tom Cody is the founder and managing partner of Project^ ecological development, a Portland-based development company. He oversees the firm's business and is involved in new business development, project planning, financing, and expanding education-related developments and other government facilities and public/private partnerships. Cody has developed numerous student housing projects, a health professions campus for Pacific University, The Civic (in Portland, Oregon), and South Park (co-developed in Los Angeles with Williams & Dame Development).

Cody has extensive experience in city planning, architecture, and development. He earned a master's degree in urban planning from Harvard University and a BS in urban planning and development from the University of Southern California. He also worked for Pritzker Prize–winning architect Frank O. Gehry and is currently the chairman of the board of trustees of Oregon Ballet Theater.

William Gilchrist
Atlanta, Georgia

William Gilchrist is a senior associate with EDAW/AECOM in Atlanta, Georgia. From 1993 to 2009, he was director of the Department of Planning, Engineering, and Permits for Birmingham, Alabama. Among other civic and professional groups, the American Institute of Architects (AIA), the American Planning Association, and the National League of Cities have honored the work of his Birmingham department.

A graduate of Massachusetts Institute of Technology (MIT)'s schools of management and architecture, with a master's degree from each, as well as a degree from Harvard's Kennedy School of Government, Gilchrist was among the first Aga Khan traveling fellows, documenting the Swahili architecture of coastal Kenya. He has chaired the committee that oversees the AIA Regional/Urban Design Assistance Teams and is a trustee of the Urban Land Institute as well as vice chairman of its executive committee. Currently, Gilchrist serves on the departmental visiting committee of the MIT School of Architecture.

Gilchrist has been interviewed on National Public Radio, has appeared on PBS's *The News Hour with Jim Lehrer*, and speaks often on urbanism, regional planning, citizen participation in the public realm, and the history of urban settlement.

Gary Hack
Philadelphia, Pennsylvania

Gary Hack is professor of urban design in the School of Design at the University of Pennsylvania. From 1996 to 2008, he served as dean of the School of Design. Before becoming dean, he was professor of urban design and head of the department of urban studies and planning at the Massachusetts Institute of Technology.

Hack has prepared plans for cities, neighborhoods, and developments in more than 35 cities in the United States, Canada, and Asia. His work includes plans for the redevelopment of Prudential Center in Boston, the transformation of the West Side Waterfront in New York, and other large-scale urban development projects. He collaborated on the winning entry in the competition for the redevelopment of the World Trade Center in New York and headed the effort of preparing urban design guidelines for the project.

He is coauthor of *Site Planning* (third edition), *Global City Regions: Their Emerging Forms*, and *Urban Design in a Global Perspective*, among other publications. He has served as the chair of the Philadelphia City Planning Commission and has been a member of many design review committees.

Educated in architecture as well as city and regional planning, Hack obtained a BArch from the University of Manitoba, Canada; an MArch from the University of Illinois; an MUP from the University of Illinois; and a PhD from Massachusetts Institute of Technology. He was awarded an honorary doctor of laws degree by Dalhousie University.

Kenneth Hughes
Dallas, Texas

Ken Hughes is CEO of Hughes Development, a Dallas-based real estate development firm. Hughes began his career with the Henry S. Miller Company in Dallas. He was with the company for 15 years, eventually becoming executive vice president and a member of the board of directors. He has served as an adviser to several foreign-based developers including Arquitectos Javier Sordo Madaleno on Moliere 333 in Mexico City; Fabrikasa in Caracas, Venezuela; and Lensworth, in Melbourne, Australia.

Hughes has served on the board of directors of the Real Estate Council in Dallas, and he served for three years on the mayor of Dallas's Inside the Loop Committee for the rebuilding of downtown Dallas. He is a continuing guest lecturer on urban housing and mixed-use development with the Real Estate Initiative at the Harvard Graduate School of Design. A member or a leader in several professional and civic organizations, he has been a trustee of the Urban Land Institute and chairman of its *The Dollars and Cents of Shopping Centers*. He currently is on the Policy and Practice Committee of ULI and is a governor of the institute.

Hughes attended the University of Texas at Austin School of Architecture and Southern Methodist University (SMU) Cox School of Business and has been a member of the advisory board of the Cox School of Business and the Meadows School of the Arts, SMU. He currently serves on and is a Life Member of the Advisory Council of the University of Texas at Austin School of Architecture.

Christopher Kurz
Baltimore, Maryland

Chris Kurz, the president of Linden Associates, has more than 30 years of commercial real estate experience. Linden Associates, Inc., is a mid-Atlantic-based real estate company that specializes in the development, acquisition, management, and financing of commercial properties from Philadelphia, Pennsylvania, to Raleigh, North Carolina.

After graduating from the Wharton School MBA program in 1971, Kurz worked for the Rouse Company. Since 1986, he has operated his own company and has developed over 950,000 square feet of office, retail, and industrial property in the Washington/Baltimore market. During his career, Kurz has developed or acquired over 2.3 million square feet of commercial real estate and has arranged financing of approximately $750 million.

Between his tenure at Rouse and starting his development company in 1986, Kurz worked for a bank, mortgage banker, and investment banking firm specializing in real estate. As a principal in the real estate affiliate of Alex. Brown & Sons (now Deutsche Bank), he represented public pension fund clients in the financing and acquisition of commercial real estate throughout the United States. He was also responsible for the firm's marketing program to pension funds. As the Baltimore regional manager for H.G. Smithy Co., Kurz represented the real estate departments of Travelers, Manulife, and other insurance companies in the Baltimore and Washington markets. He was hired from Rouse by a regional bank in the mid-1970s to work out a portfolio of troubled assets.

David Malmuth
San Diego, California

David Malmuth established David Malmuth Development, a real estate development firm focused on the creation of art-inspired places that transform communities, in 2010. Before starting his own firm, Malmuth was the founder and managing director for seven years with RCLCO's Development Services Group. Malmuth drew upon his 25 years of experience in the development business, which included completion as principal developer of over $1 billion in high-profile projects, to assist numerous clients in the planning and execution of mixed-use, entertainment, and waterfront developments. Clients included Rockefeller Group, Kamehameha Schools, MGM MIRAGE, and the sponsor of the "Imagine Coney" charette, the Municipal Art Society.

From 1996 to 2002, Malmuth was a senior vice president at TrizecHahn Development Corporation. Before TrizecHahn, he was vice president/general manager at Disney Development Company–West. During his nine years at the Walt Disney Company, Malmuth managed the development of over $200 million in projects, including the Feature Animation Building in Burbank (with architect Robert A.M. Stern) and Disney Ice in Anaheim (with architect Frank Gehry).

Malmuth received his MBA from Stanford University and his BA from Claremont McKenna College. He is a member of the Urban Land Institute's Policy and Practice Committee and a founding board member of Disney Goals, a nonprofit entity that provides underserved Anaheim youth with positive options through sports, academic training, and community service.

Randall Rowe
Lake Forest, Illinois

Randy Rowe is chairman of Green Courte Partners, LLC, a Chicago-based private-equity real estate investment firm focused on niche real estate strategies, including the acquisition and development of manufactured-housing community, parking, and infill retail (mixed-use) assets. Previously, Rowe was a cofounder and chairman of Transwestern Investment Company, LLC, and chairman and director of Transwestern Commercial Services, LLC. He was also chairman and CEO of Hometown America, LLC, a large owner of manufactured-housing communities.

Rowe is a trustee of the Urban Land Institute. He is also a member of the advisory board of the Real Estate Academic Initiative at Harvard University, the board of the Primo Center for Women and Children, the board of trustees of the Steppenwolf Theatre and a member and former chairman of the Real Estate Roundtable.

He holds a BA from Denison University, an MBA from Harvard University, and a JD from the University of Michigan. Rowe is a member of the State Bar of Illinois.

John Slidell
Greenbelt, Maryland

A cofounder and principal of the Bozzuto Group, John Slidell is also currently president of Bozzuto Land Company where he directs the acquisition and development of land for both the company's homebuilding and apartment operations and third-party sales. He has been responsible for the development of more than 6,000 apartment units and led the growth of the company's homebuilding operation to an average volume of 250 starts, with increasing emphasis on mixed-use properties with close-in urban and suburban infill locations.

Before the formation of Bozzuto in 1988, Slidell spent six years as a vice president and operating partner for Oxford Development Company, where he was involved with the development of more than 7,100 apartment units in the mid-Atlantic region. He has also worked as a partner with Zuchelli Hunter & Associates, a real estate consulting firm specializing in mixed-use public/private partnership development, and for Mitchell Energy and Development Company, developer of the Woodlands community in Houston, Texas.

A graduate of Princeton University, Slidell has a master's in city and regional planning from the University of North Carolina. He is currently a counselor for the Urban Land Institute's four Residential Councils, immediate past chair of ULI's Residential Neighborhood Development Council, and a member of the Executive Committee of ULI's Washington District Council. He is also a life director of the Northern Virginia Building Industry Association and the Montgomery Housing Partnership. In addition to industry leadership, Slidell has been active in many community organizations including serving as board chair of the Severn School and the Bethesda Cultural Alliance.

Rebecca R. Zimmermann
Denver, Colorado

Becky Zimmermann is a partner and the president of Design Workshop, an international land planning, urban design, and strategic services firm. She is highly recognized for her work with resort communities, including development strategy, market definition, positioning, and tourism planning; and in urban areas for brownfield redevelopment, development entitlements, and real estate economics. She is a frequent keynote speaker at conferences, including the Union of British Columbia Municipalities Conference on Sustainability, the ULI Recreation Development Council, and ULI Real Estate School. Her work has been published in *Metropolis*, *Landscape Architecture*, and *Urban Land* magazines.

Zimmermann holds an MBA from the University of Colorado, Denver, as well as bachelor's degrees in both communications and business administration from Trinity University in San Antonio, Texas. She is a member of the Young Presidents' Organization, serves on the Riverfront Park Community Foundation board of directors, and is on the board of trustees for the National Sports Center for the Disabled.

EMEA Jury

Ian D. Hawksworth, Jury Chair
London, United Kingdom

Ian Hawksworth is the managing director of Capital & Counties and an executive director of Liberty International PLC. Liberty International is a leading FTSE-100 ranking U.K.-listed real estate investment trust with property investments of over £8.2 billion. Through its two principal subsidiaries, Capital & Counties and Capital Shopping Centres, the group focuses on premier property assets that have scarcity value and require active management and creativity.

Previously, Hawksworth worked in Asia for 14 years. Based in Hong Kong, he was an executive director of Hongkong Land with responsibilities in commercial property and development.

Hawksworth has a BS in estate management and is a member of the Royal Institution of Chartered Surveyors. He is a trustee of the Urban Land Institute, participates in the Harvard Real Estate Academic Initiative, and is a member of the British Property Federation Policy Committee.

Max Barclay
Stockholm, Sweden

Max Barclay has over 20 years of experience working in the Nordic region's real estate industry. Starting at an early age in Gothenburg, Barclay has extensive experience as an international adviser on corporate real estate and strategic real estate issues within Newsec and is now responsible for the Stronghold Group's international expansion and communication, covering all subsidiaries. Barclay is chairman of the board of Stronghold's Norwegian, Finnish, Estonian, Latvian, and Lithuanian companies, Newsec AS Eiendoms-Consult, Newsec Oy, and Re&Solution.

He is one of the principal owners of Stronghold Invest AB. With 18 offices in seven countries, the Stronghold Group comprises three companies—Newsec, Niam, and Datscha—with more than 600 employees. The Stronghold Group's history is a success story with 30 percent annual growth over a period of 12 years.

Andrew Gould
London, United Kingdom

Andrew Gould is chief executive of the Jones Lang LaSalle business in England.

Over the last 25 years, Gould has advised on many of the large-scale urban regeneration projects in the United Kingdom and continental Europe. His projects included Greenwich Peninsula, where he was commercial adviser to the government on the successful sale of the Millennium Dome as the anchor for a 1.3 million-square-meter (14 million-sf) multiuse urban regeneration program and on various aspects of the London 2012 Olympics site. He has advised many leading corporate and real estate investors on their asset strategies and governmental and public institutions on urban regeneration and economic development.

Gould has a PhD from the University of Cambridge, where he taught, and a Corporate Finance Diploma from London Business School.

Hakan Kodal
Istanbul, Turkey

Since 2006, Hakan Kodal has been president and CEO of Istanbul-based Krea Real Estate. He is also chairman of the Investment Committee of Bosphorus Real Estate Fund, jointly managed by Merrill Lynch GPI and Krea Real Estate. Between 1997 and 2007, Kodal was general manager of Yapı Kredi Koray Real Estate Investment Company. Before 1997, he worked as a corporate finance manager at Garanti Investment Bank, Istanbul. Between 1991 and 1995, he held various positions at Coopers & Lybrand, Corporate Finance, in Paris.

Kodal holds a BS in electronics and telecommunication from Istanbul Technical University and a graduate degree from the École Supérieure de Commerce de Paris. He is the founding chairman of the Council of Shopping Centers–Turkey (AYD) and the National Association of Turkish Real Estate Investment Companies (GYODER), a global trustee of the Urban Land Institute, and founding chairman of ULI Turkey.

Karsten von Köller
Frankfurt, Germany

Karsten von Köller was elected to the board of directors of W.P. Carey & Co. LLC in December 2003. He is currently chairman of Lone Star Germany GmbH, deputy chairman of the supervisory board of Corealcredit Bank AG, deputy chairman of the Supervisory Board of MHB Bank AG, and vice chairman of the Supervisory Board of IKB Deutsche Industriebank AG. He was chairman of the board of management of Eurohypo AG until December 2003, and from 1984 through 2001 he was a member of the board of managing directors of Rheinhyp Rheinische Hypothekenbank AG (Commerzbank group), where he was responsible for the bank's commercial real estate lending activities outside Germany. Von Köller was an executive vice president of Berliner Handels-und Frankfurter Bank (BHF-BANK), Frankfurt, and was responsible for the bank's corporate customer business in northern and western Germany and in western industrial countries from 1981 through 1984. Before holding this position, from 1977 through 1980, he served as senior vice president and comanager of the New York branch of BHF-BANK.

Von Köller studied law at the universities of Bonn and Munich and is a graduate of Harvard Business School.

Raj Menda
Bangalore, India

Raj Menda is the managing director of RMZ Corp, a leading commercial and residential real estate company in India. RMZ, founded in 2002 by Menda and his family, has developed more than 1.2 million square meters (13 million sf) of Class A office space in Bangalore, Hyderabad, Chennai, Kolkata, and Pune. Its first green building was the first office building in India to receive a LEED-Platinum certification. At RMZ, Menda is responsible for sourcing funds, striking deals, and developing and managing office, residential, retail, and hospitality properties.

Menda earned a graduate degree in commerce and business management. He is the honorary secretary of the National Real Estate Developers Association, which is a constituent part of the Confederation of Real Estate Developers Association of India, past Honorary Secretary of the National Confederation of Real Estate Developers Association of India, in 2009 chairman of the ULI Asia Pacific Awards, an active member of the Global Real Estate Institute and the Urban Land Institute, and a founding member of the Bangalore chapter of the Young Presidents' Organization.

Luca de Ambrosis Ortigara
Milan, Italy

Luca de Ambrosis Ortigara is CEO and partner of DEA Real Estate Advisor, which focuses on high-level retail premises, commercial services, and strategic advisory services for prime customers' property assets. He is also a founding partner of Realty Partners, an Italian real estate management and strategic advisory firm (2004) focusing on five areas: strategic consulting, asset management, real estate fund management, commercial services, and equity investment. Among its clients are Credit Suisse, Caisse de Dépôt et Placement du Québec, First Boston, Gruppo Fondiaria, Aedes, Pirelli RE, and Deka. Previously, he worked with McArthurGlen as CEO for Italy and group commercial director for Europe. He has also worked at Pirelli Real Estate as director of real estate services and was a partner in Cushman and Wakefield.

Ortigara is chair of Urban Land Institute Italy and a member of the executive committee of MAPIC. He also sits on the Scientific and Retail Executive Committee of Expo Italia Real Estate. He has been a visiting professor for the master's degree course in Fashion, Experience, and Design at the SDA Bocconi University in Milan.

Asia Pacific Jury

Nicholas Brooke, Jury Chair
Hong Kong, China

Nicholas Brooke is the chairman of Professional Property Services Limited, a specialist real estate consultancy based in Hong Kong, providing a selected range of advisory services across the Asia Pacific region. Having spent the last 25 years based in the region, Brooke is a recognized authority and commentator on property-related and planning matters and has provided advice in these areas to several Asian governments as well as the U.S. State Department.

He is a past president of the Royal Institution of Chartered Surveyors and a former member of the Hong Kong Housing Authority and the Hong Kong Town Planning Board. Currently, Brooke is chairman of the Hong Kong Science and Technology Park Corporation and of the Hong Kong Coalition of Service Industries as well as a member of the Hong Kong Harbourfront Enhancement Committee.

Brooke is a nonexecutive director on the board of MAF Properties, one of the Middle East's leading shopping center developers; of Vinaland Vietnam Real Estate Fund, the first Vietnamese property fund to be listed on the AIM board of the London Stock Exchange; of Shanghai Forte Land, one of the largest residential developers in mainland China; and of China Central Properties Limited, another AIM-listed mainland property development company.

Mark Fogle
Hong Kong, China

Mark Fogle is the managing director for Asia Pacific Infrastructure and chief investment officer of RREEF Asia, based in Singapore. Fogle joined RREEF in 2007 and has more than 25 years of asset management and investment experience, 15 of which have been spent in the Asia Pacific region. RREEF has $62.4 billion in assets under management globally and focuses on investments in real estate, infrastructure, and private equity. RREEF Asia's real estate business has $1.6 billion in assets under management.

From 1997 to 2006, Fogle was a managing director of AIG Global Investment Corp., the investment arm of American International Group, Inc. Prior to joining AIG, he was responsible for the Asian expansion of the John Buck Company, a U.S. development and service firm.

Ross Holt
Perth, Australia

Ross Holt is chief executive of LandCorp, a government trading enterprise that operates as the Western Australia government's specialist property development agency. LandCorp provides a commercially oriented vehicle for delivering the state's strategic land development goals.

LandCorp's professional staff provides a diverse set of property development services, including property acquisition and planning, business administration, and strategic marketing, helping LandCorp operate with a triple-bottom-line approach. Over half of its more than 200 projects throughout the state are located outside the capital city of Perth.

Under Holt's leadership, LandCorp has focused on sustainable development outcomes for the benefit of the affected community. It has sought to extend those outcomes to the built form through the application of design and building guidelines and through joint ventures with private sector development and building entities.

Holt graduated from the University of Western Australia with an honors degree in economics. Prior to joining LandCorp in 1993, he held a senior position in the state's treasury department.

Paul Husband
Hong Kong, China

Paul Husband is managing director of Husband Retail Consulting, a global consulting firm with experience in innovative retail center planning, place making, marketing, and leasing for international clients wishing to maximize their retail asset growth. Husband Retail Consulting has more than ten years of global and Asia-specific experience working with international real estate developers on successful iconic projects and luxury shopping centers worldwide. A native of the United Kingdom, Husband launched his career as marketing manager for Pacific Place in Hong Kong, one of Asia's most successful and high-profile retail centers.

Husband is also an Asian faculty member of the International Council of Shopping Centers and a member of the Urban Land Institute and is frequently invited to speak at key conferences and seminars around the world, particularly in relation to future luxury retail trends across China, India, and throughout Asia. In 2006, he made his debut as an author, with the launch of *The Cult of the Luxury Brand*.

Hokyu Lee
Seoul, Korea

Hokyu Lee was appointed chairman of Savills Korea in July 2009. Before taking a role as chairman, Lee was appointed as both Savills Asia Pacific Executive Member in 2006 and Representative of Savills Korea and was responsible for overseeing Korea's operations comprising some 150 staff in two cities, Seoul and Busan.

In 1994, Lee founded BHP Korea as the first international property-consulting firm in Korea, providing a comprehensive scope of services related to all aspects of real estate development, investment, transactions, operation, valuation, asset management, and marketing and overseas investment. In 1999, Lee also founded Korea Asset Advisors, a real estate asset management company. The company was a leader in the market, managing 27 properties with more than 1 million square meters (11 million sf) under its property and asset management with leasing-marketing.

Lee graduated from Columbia University with a master's of architecture in urban design in 1988.

S. C. Liu
Hong Kong, China

S. C. Liu is the chairman of My Top Home (China) Holdings Ltd. and Evergreen Real Estate Consultants Ltd., which provide a host of integrated real estate related services in China. He is a member of the Council of Hong Kong University of Science and Technology (HKUST), the Development Committee under the West Kowloon Cultural District Authority, and the board of directors of Hong Kong Science and Technology Parks Corporation. Liu is an independent nonexecutive director of Swire Properties Limited.

He was conferred an Honorary Fellowship of the HKUST and Outstanding Hong Kong Polytechnic University Alumni Award. He was the founding chairman of the Asia Pacific Board of the Royal Institution of Chartered Surveyors.

Tomohisa Miyauchi
Tokyo, Japan

Tomohisa Miyauchi is a partner at ISSHO Architects, a Tokyo design firm that he cofounded after graduating from the Harvard Graduate School of Design and the Southern California Institute of Architecture. The firm designs a large variety of projects, including houses, apartments, offices, boutiques, hotels, and mixed-use spaces. The firm works both locally in Tokyo and increasingly abroad, with projects in China, such as a pavilion at the 2010 Shanghai Expo and a fashion boutique.

Miyauchi is responsible for representing the company; interacting with clients, among whom are developers and landowners; and collaborating with professionals from different fields. He also developed ISSHO's philosophy of humanistic architecture, focusing on personal involvement in community on both neighborhood and global levels and collaboration between diverse experts. He belongs to the Tokyo Society of Architects & Building Engineers and the American Institute of Architects and is a senior editor of *Architecture + Urbanism* magazine.

Rocco Yim
Hong Kong, China

Rocco Yim founded his own practice in 1979, and was one of the cofounders of Rocco Design Partners in 1982. The firm has received many local and international awards and citations for design excellence since its inception and won its first international competition in 1983. Recent accolades include ARCASIA Gold Medals in 1994 and 2003, the Chicago Athenaeum Architectural Award in 2006, the Kenneth F. Brown Award in 2007, and winning designs through international competitions for the Guangdong Museum in 2004, and the Hong Kong special administrative region Government Headquarters at Tamar in 2007. Under his stewardship in design, the firm has grown significantly over the years in both size and reputation. Yim is also an honorary professor at the Hong Kong University Department of Architecture and a museum adviser to the Leisure and Cultural Services Department of Hong Kong.

Yim is regularly invited to speak at international symposia and seminars, such as the ARCASIA Forum, the IAA Symposia, and the Harvard Graduate School of Design Conference and New Trends Architecture 2005. His work has been published in such regional and international journals as *SD*, *SPACE*, *AR*, *Zoo*, *ROOT*, *Domus*, *Frames*, *Art in America*, and *Architectural Review*. He graduated from the University of Hong Kong in 1979.

The following 289 projects have received ULI Awards for Excellence. Each project name is followed by its location and its developer/owner.

1979
First year of award
The Galleria; Houston, Texas; Hines Interests Limited Partnership

1980
Charles Center; Baltimore, Maryland; Baltimore City Development Corporation

1981
WDW/Reedy Creek; Orlando, Florida; The Walt Disney Company

1982
Two awards given: large and small scale
Large Scale: Heritage Village; Southbury, Connecticut; Heritage Development Group, Inc. • Small Scale: Promontory Point; Newport Beach, California; The Irvine Company

1983
Large Scale: Eaton Centre; Toronto, Canada; Cadillac Fairview Limited

1984
Large Scale: Embarcadero Center; San Francisco, California; Embarcadero Center, Ltd. • Small Scale: Rainbow Centre; Niagara Falls, New York; The Cordish Company

1985
Introduction of product categories
New Community: Las Colinas; Irving, Texas; JPI Partners, Inc. • Large-Scale Residential: Museum Tower; New York, New York; The Charles H. Shaw Company • Small-Scale Urban Mixed Use: Sea Colony Condominiums; Santa Monica, California; Dominion Property Company • Large-Scale Recreational: Sea Pines Plantation; Hilton Head, South Carolina; Community Development Institute • Small-Scale Urban Mixed Use: Vista Montoya; Los Angeles, California; Pico Union Neighborhood Council/Community Redevelopment Agency

1986
Introduction of rehabilitation and special categories
Small-Scale Mixed Use: 2000 Pennsylvania Avenue; Washington, D.C.; George Washington University • Small-Scale Rehabilitation: Downtown Costa Mesa; Costa Mesa, California; PSB Realty Corporation • Special: Inner Harbor Shoreline; Baltimore, Maryland; Baltimore City Development Corporation • Large-Scale Recreational: Kaanapali Beach Resort; Kaanapali, Hawaii; Amfac/JMB Hawaii • Large-Scale Residential: The Landings on Skidaway Island; Savannah, Georgia; The Bramigar Organization, Inc. • Small-Scale Industrial/Office Park: The Purdue Frederick Company; Norwalk, Connecticut; The Purdue Frederick Company • Large-Scale Recreational: Water Tower Place; Chicago, Illinois; JMB Realty Corporation

1987
Large-Scale Industrial/Office Park: Bishop Ranch Business Park; San Ramon, California; Sunset Development Company • Small-Scale Commercial/Retail: Loews Ventana Canyon Resort; Tucson, Arizona; Estes Homebuilding • Large-Scale Urban Mixed Use: St. Louis Union Station; St. Louis, Missouri; The Rouse Company • Small-Scale Residential: Straw Hill; Manchester, New Hampshire; George Matarazzo and Mark Stebbins • Rehabilitation: The Willard Inter-Continental; Washington, D.C.; The Oliver Carr Company

1988
Large-Scale Urban Mixed Use: Copley Place; Boston, Massachusetts; Urban Investment & Development Company • Special: Downtown Women's Center; Los Angeles, California; The Ratkovich Company • Large-Scale Commercial/Retail: The Grand Avenue; Milwaukee, Wisconsin; Milwaukee Redevelopment Corporation (MRC) • Rehabilitation: Northpoint; Chicago, Illinois; Amoco Neighborhood Development • Small-Scale Residential: Pickleweed Apartments; Mill Valley, California; BRIDGE Housing Corporation • Large-Scale Residential: Rector Place; New York, New York; Battery Park City Authority • Small-Scale Office: Wilshire Palisades; Santa Monica, California; Tooley & Company

1989
Introduction of Heritage Award

Small-Scale Urban Mixed Use: Charleston Place; Charleston, South Carolina; The Taubman Company, Inc., and Cordish Embry Associates (joint venture) • Rehabilitation: Commonwealth Development; Boston, Massachusetts; Corcoran Management • Small-Scale Office: Escondido City Hall; Escondido, California; City of Escondido • Large-Scale Office: Norwest Center; Minneapolis, Minnesota; Hines Interests • Special: Pratt-Willert Neighborhood; Buffalo, New York; City of Buffalo • New Community: Reston; Reston, Virginia; Mobil Land Development in Virginia • **Heritage Award: Rockefeller Center**; New York, New York; The Rockefeller Group • Large-Scale Urban Mixed Use: Rowes Wharf; Boston, Massachusetts; The Beacon Companies

1990
Small-Scale Commercial: The Boulders; Carefree, Arizona; Westcor Partners • Large-Scale Industrial: Carnegie Center; Princeton, New Jersey; Carnegie Center Associates • Small-Scale Residential: Columbia Place; San Diego, California; Odmark & Thelan • Large-Scale Residential: River Run; Boise, Idaho; O'Neill Enterprises, Inc. • Special: Tent City; Boston, Massachusetts; Tent City Corporation • Rehabilitation: Wayne County Building; Detroit, Michigan; Farbman Stein • New Community: Woodlake; Richmond, Virginia; East West Partners of Virginia

1991
Small-Scale Commercial/Retail: Del Mar Plaza; Del Mar, California; Del Mar Partnership • Large-Scale Urban Mixed Use: Fashion Centre at Pentagon City; Arlington, Virginia; Melvin Simon & Associates and Rose Associates • Small-Scale Urban Mixed Use: Garibaldi Square; Chicago, Illinois; The Charles H. Shaw Company • Large-Scale Residential: Ghent Square; Norfolk, Virginia; Norfolk Redevelopment and Housing Authority • Special: Grand Central Partnership; New York, New York; Grand Central Partnership • Small-Scale Office: James R. Mills Building; San Diego, California; Starboard Development Corporation • Rehabilitation: Marina Village; Alameda, California; Vintage Properties • Special: Union Station; Washington, D.C.; Union Station Redevelopment Corporation

1992
Small-Scale Commercial/Retail: CocoWalk; Miami, Florida; Constructa U.S. • Special: The Coeur d'Alene Resort Golf Course; Coeur d'Alene, Idaho; Hagadone Hospitality • Special: The Delancey Street Foundation; San Francisco, California; The Delancey Street Foundation • Public: Harbor Point; Boston, Massachusetts; Corcoran Jennison Companies • Large-Scale Mixed Use: Market Square; Washington, D.C.; Trammell Crow • New Community: Planned Community of Mission Viejo; Mission Viejo, California; Mission Viejo Company • Small-Scale Residential: Summit Place; St. Paul, Minnesota; Robert Engstrom Companies • Rehabilitation: Tysons Corner Center; McLean, Virginia; The L&B Group

1993
Small-Scale Residential: Beverly Hills Senior Housing; Beverly Hills, California; Jewish Federation Council • Special: Charlestown Navy Yard; Charlestown, Massachusetts; Boston Redevelopment Authority • **Heritage Award: The Country Club Plaza**; Kansas City, Missouri; J.C. Nichols Company • Large-Scale Residential: The Cypress of Hilton Head Island; Hilton Head Island, South Carolina; The Melrose Company • Small-Scale Rehabilitation: Furness House; Baltimore, Maryland; The Cordish Company • Large-Scale Recreational: Kapalua; Kapalua, Maui, Hawaii; Kapalua Land Company, Ltd. • Special: Post

Office Square Park and Garage; Boston, Massachusetts; Friends of Post Office Square, Inc. • Rehabilitation: Schlitz Park; Milwaukee, Wisconsin; The Brewery Works, Inc. • Small-Scale Commercial/Retail: The Somerset Collection; Troy, Michigan; Forbes/Cohen Properties and Frankel Associates

1994
Introduction of international category

International: Broadgate; London, United Kingdom; Stanhope Properties • Small-Scale Residential: Orchard Village; Chattanooga, Tennessee; Chattanooga Neighborhood Enterprise • Public: Oriole Park at Camden Yards; Baltimore, Maryland; Maryland Stadium Authority • Special: The Pennsylvania Avenue Plan; Washington, D.C.; Pennsylvania Avenue Development Corporation • Large-Scale Rehabilitation: Phipps Plaza; Atlanta, Georgia; Compass Retail, Inc. • **Heritage Award: Sea Pines Plantation**; Hilton Head Island, South Carolina; Charles Fraser • Large-Scale Office: Washington Mutual Tower; Seattle, Washington; Wright Runstad and Company • Large-Scale Residential: Woodbridge; Irvine, California; The Irvine Company • Special: The Woodlands; The Woodlands, Texas; The Woodlands Corporation

1995
Small-Scale Rehabilitation: 640 Memorial Drive; Cambridge, Massachusetts; Massachusetts Institute of Technology Real Estate • Large-Scale Commercial/Retail: Broadway Plaza; Walnut Creek, California; Macerich Northwestern Associates and The Macerich Company • **Heritage Award: Disneyland Park**; Anaheim, California; The Walt Disney Company • Large-Scale Industrial/Office: Irvine Spectrum; Orange County, California; The Irvine Company • Small-Scale Recreational: Little Nell Hotel and Aspen Mountain Base; Aspen, Colorado; Aspen Skiing Company • Special: Monterey Bay Aquarium; Monterey, California; The Monterey Bay Aquarium Foundation • New Community: Pelican Bay; Naples, Florida; WCI Communities LP • Special: Riverbank State Park; New York, New York; New York State Office of Parks, Recreation and Historic Preservation • Small-Scale Residential: Strathern Park Apartments; Sun Valley, California; Thomas Safran and Associates

1996
Large-Scale Residential: Avenel; Potomac, Maryland; Natelli Communities • Public: Bryant Park; New York, New York; Bryant Park Restoration Corporation • Large-Scale Office: Comerica Tower at Detroit Center; Detroit, Michigan; Hines Interests Limited Partnership • Small-Scale Residential: The Court Home Collection at Valencia NorthPark; Valencia, California; The Newhall Land and Farming Company, and RGC • Small-Scale Commercial/Hotel: The Forum Shops; Las Vegas, Nevada; Simon Property Group • Small-Scale Mixed Use: The Heritage on the Garden; Boston, Massachusetts; The Druker Company • Large-Scale Recreational: Kiawah Island; Kiawah Island, South Carolina; Kiawah Resort Associates LP • Special: The Scattered Site Program; Chicago, Illinois; The Habitat Company

1997
Heritage Award: The Arizona Biltmore Hotel and Resort; Phoenix, Arizona; Grossman Company Properties • Rehabilitation: Chelsea Piers; New York, New York; Chelsea Piers LP • Large-Scale Recreational: Desert Mountain; Scottsdale, Arizona; Desert Mountain Properties • Rehabilitation: Eagles Building Restoration; Seattle, Washington; A Contemporary Theater and Housing Resources Group (general partners) • Small-Scale Residential: Mercado Apartments; San Diego, California; City of San Diego Redevelopment Agency • Large-Scale Commercial/Hotel: Park Meadows; Park Meadows, Colorado; TrizecHahn Centers • Special: Pennsylvania Convention Center; Philadelphia, Pennsylvania; Pennsylvania

Convention Center Authority • Special: A Safe House for Kids and Moms; Irvine, California; Human Options • Public: Smyrna Town Center; Smyrna, Georgia; City of Smyrna, Knight-Davidson Companies (residential) and Thomas Enterprises (retail/offices) • International: Stockley Park at Heathrow; Uxbridge, Middlesex, United Kingdom; Stanhope Properties PLC

1998
Large-Scale Business Park: Alliance; Fort Worth, Texas; Hillwood Development Corporation • Special: American Visionary Art Museum; Baltimore, Maryland; Rebecca and LeRoy E. Hoffberger • International: Calakmul; Mexico City, Mexico; Francisco G. Coronado (owner) • Small-Scale Residential: Courthouse Hill; Arlington, Virginia; Eakin/Youngentob Associates, Inc. • Public: Harold Washington Library Center; Chicago, Illinois; U.S. Equities Realty (developer) • Special: Richmond City Center; Richmond, California; BRIDGE Housing Corporation (owner) • Rehabilitation: Twenty-Eight State Street; Boston, Massachusetts; Equity Office Properties Trust • Rehabilitation: UtiliCorp United World Headquarters/New York Life Building; Kansas City, Missouri; The Zimmer Companies • Small-Scale Recreational: Village Center; Beaver Creek, Colorado; East West Partners

1999
Small-Scale Rehabilitation: Bayou Place; Houston, Texas; The Cordish Company • Large-Scale Residential: Bonita Bay; Bonita Springs, Florida; Bonita Bay Properties Inc. • Public: Chicago Public Schools Capital Improvement Program; Chicago, Illinois; Chicago Public Schools • Small-Scale Commercial/Hotel: The Commons at Calabasas; Calabasas, California; Caruso Affiliated Holdings • Special: Coors Field; Denver, Colorado; Denver Metropolitan Stadium District • Small-Scale Mixed Use: East Pointe; Milwaukee, Wisconsin; Milwaukee Redevelopment Corporation and Mandel Group Inc. • Large-Scale Recreational: Hualalai; Ka'upulehu-Kona, Hawaii; Ka'upulehu Makai Venture/Hualalai Development Company • Large-Scale Rehabilitation: John Hancock Center; Chicago, Illinois; U.S. Equities Realty • Small-Scale Residential: Normandie Village; Los Angeles, California; O.N.E. Company Inc. and SIPA (general partners) • Small-Scale Commercial/Hotel: Seventh & Collins Parking Facility (Ballet Valet); Miami Beach, Florida; City of Miami Beach, Goldman Properties • International: Vinohradský Pavilon; Prague, Czech Republic; Prague Investment, a.s.

2000
Small-Scale Rehabilitation: Amazon.com Building; Seattle, Washington; Wright Runstad and Company • Heritage Award: The Burnham Plan; Chicago, Illinois; The Commercial Club of Chicago • Small-Scale Residential: The Colony; Newport Beach, California; Irvine Apartment Communities • Large-Scale Residential: Coto de Caza; Orange County, California; Lennar Communities • Small-Scale Mixed Use: DePaul Center; Chicago, Illinois; DePaul University • Public: NorthLake Park Community School; Orlando, Florida; Lake Nona Land Company • Large-Scale Rehabilitation: The Power Plant; Baltimore, Maryland; The Cordish Company • International: Sony Center am Potsdamer Platz; Berlin, Germany; Tishman Speyer Properties, Sony Corporation, Kajima Corporation, and BE-ST Development GmbH & Co. (owner) • Special: Spring Island; Beaufort County, South Carolina; Chaffin/Light Associates • Public: The Townhomes on Capitol Hill; Washington, D.C.; Ellen Wilson CDC and Telesis Corporation • Large-Scale Recreational: Whistler Village/Blackcomb Benchlands; Whistler, British Columbia, Canada; Resort Municipality of Whistler, and INTRAWEST Corporation

2001
International category eliminated

New Community: Celebration; Celebration, Florida; The Celebration Company • Special: Dewees Island; Dewees Island, South Carolina; Island Preservation Partnership • Large-Scale Residential: Harbor Steps; Seattle, Washington; Harbor Properties Inc. • Small-Scale Rehabilitation; Pier 1; San Francisco, California; AMB Property Corporation • Small-Scale Recreational: The Reserve; Indian Wells, California; Lowe Enterprises Inc. • Small-Scale Office: Thames Court; London, United Kingdom; Markborough Properties Limited • Special: Townhomes at Oxon Creek; Washington, D.C.; William C. Smith & Company Inc. • Large-Scale Mixed Use: Valencia Town Center Drive; Valencia, California; The Newhall Land and Farming Company • Large-Scale Commercial/Hotel: The Venetian Casino Resort; Las Vegas, Nevada; LVS/Development Group • Public: Yerba Buena Gardens; San Francisco, California; Yerba Buena Alliance

2002
Small-Scale Mixed Use: Bethesda Row; Bethesda, Maryland; Federal Realty Investment Trust • Large-Scale Mixed Use: CityPlace; West Palm Beach, Florida; The Related Companies • Special: Envision Utah; Salt Lake City, Utah; Coalition for Utah's Future • Public: Homan Square Community Center Campus; Chicago, Illinois; Homan Square Community Center Foundation (owner) and The Shaw Company (developer) • Small-Scale Rehabilitation: Hotel Burnham at the Reliance Building; Chicago, Illinois; McCaffery Interests • Special: Memphis Ballpark District; Memphis, Tennessee; Memphis Redbirds Foundation (owner), and Parkway Properties Inc. (developer) • Large-Scale Office: One Raffles Link; Singapore Central, Singapore; Hongkong Land Property Co. Ltd. • Small-Scale Rehabilitation: REI Denver Flagship Store; Denver, Colorado; Recreational Equipment Inc. • Large-Scale Recreational: Station Mont Tremblant; Quebec, Canada; Intrawest • New Community: Summerlin North; Las Vegas, Nevada; The Rouse Company

2003
Product categories eliminated

Atago Green Hills; Tokyo, Japan; Mori Building Company • Ayala Center Greenbelt 3; Makati City, Manila, Philippines; Ayala Land Inc. • Bay Harbor; Bay Harbor, Michigan; Victor International Corporation • Chattahoochee River Greenway; Georgia; Chattahoochee River Coordinating Committee • The Grove and Farmers Market; Los Angeles, California; Caruso Affiliated Holdings (The Grove), and A.F. Gilmore Company (Farmers Market) • Millennium Place; Boston, Massachusetts; Millennium Partners/MDA Associates • Shanghai Xintiandi (North Block); Shanghai, China; Shui On Group • The Town of Seaside; Seaside, Florida; Seaside Community Development Corporation • The Villages of East Lake; Atlanta, Georgia; East Lake Community Foundation Inc. • The West Philadelphia Initiatives; Philadelphia, Pennsylvania; University of Pennsylvania

2004 The Americas and Asia Pacific
Baldwin Park; Orlando, Florida; Baldwin Park Development Company • Fall Creek Place; Indianapolis, Indiana; City of Indiana (owner), Mansur Real Estate Services Inc., and King Park Area Development Corporation (developers) • First Ward Place/The Garden District; Charlotte, North Carolina; City of Charlotte (owner), Banc of America Community Development Corporation (master developer) • The Fullerton Square Project; Singapore; Far East Organization/Sino Land • Playhouse Square Center; Cleveland, Ohio; Playhouse Square Foundation • The Plaza at PPL Center; Allentown, Pennsylvania; Liberty Property Trust • Technology Square at Georgia Institute of Technology;

Atlanta, Georgia; Georgia Institute of Technology and Georgia Tech Foundation (owners), Jones Lang LaSalle (development manager) • University Park at MIT; Cambridge, Massachusetts; Forest City Enterprises, City of Cambridge Community Development Department, and Massachusetts Institute of Technology • Walt Disney Concert Hall; Los Angeles, California; Los Angeles County (owner), Walt Disney Concert Hall Inc. (developer) • WaterColor; Seagrove Beach, Florida; The St. Joe Company

2004 Europe
Introduction of separate European awards program

Brindleyplace; Birmingham, United Kingdom; Argent Group PLC • Bullring; Birmingham, United Kingdom; The Birmingham Alliance • Casa de les Punxes; Barcelona, Spain; Inmobiliaria Colonial • Diagonal Mar; Barcelona, Spain; Hines Interests España • Promenaden Hauptbahnhof Leipzig; Leipzig, Germany; ECE Projektmanagement GmbH & Co., Deutsche Bahn AG, and DB Immobilienfonds • Regenboogpark; Tilburg, The Netherlands; AM Wonen

2005 The Americas
34th Street Streetscape Program; New York, New York; 34th Street Partnership • 731 Lexington Avenue/One Beacon Court; New York, New York; Vornado Realty Trust • **Heritage Award: The Chautauqua Institution**; Chautauqua, New York; The Chautauqua Institution • Fourth Street Live!; Louisville, Kentucky; The Cordish Company • The Glen; Glenview, Illinois; The Village of Glenview and Mesirow Stein Real Estate Inc. • Harbor Town; Memphis, Tennessee; Henry Turley Company and Belz Enterprises • The Market Common, Clarendon; Arlington, Virginia; McCaffery Interests Inc. • **Millennium Park**; Chicago, Illinois; City of Chicago and Millennium Park Inc. • Pueblo del Sol; Los Angeles, California; The Related Companies of California, McCormack Baron Salazar, The Lee Group, and Housing Authority of the City of Los Angeles • Time Warner Center; New York, New York; The Related Companies LP • Ville Plácido Domingo; Acapulco, Mexico; Casas Geo and CIDECO-Anáhuac

2005 Europe
Cézanne Saint-Honoré; Paris, France; Société Foncière Lyonnaise and Predica • Danube House; Prague, Czech Republic; Europolis Real Estate Asset • Government Offices Great George Street; London, United Kingdom; Stanhope PLC and Bovis Lend Lease • De Hoftoren; The Hague, The Netherlands; ING Real Estate Development • Meander; Amsterdam, The Netherlands; Het Oosten Kristal and Latei

2005 Asia Pacific
Introduction of separate Asia Pacific awards program

Federation Square; Melbourne, Australia; Federation Square Management • **Hangzhou Waterfront**; Hangzhou, China; Hangzhou Hubin Commerce & Tourism Company Ltd. • The Loft; Singapore; CapitaLand Residential Ltd. • **Marunouchi Building**; Tokyo, Japan; Mitsubishi Estate Company Ltd. • Pier 6/7, Walsh Bay; Sydney, Australia; Mirvac Group and Transfield Holdings Pty Ltd.

2006 The Americas
Belmar; Lakewood, Colorado; Continuum Partners LLC, McStain neighborhoods, and Trammell Crow Residential • Ladera Ranch; Orange County, California; Rancho Mission Viejo and DMB Consolidated Holdings LLC • Los Angeles Unified School District Construction Program; Los Angeles, California; Los Angeles Unified School District • Mesa Arts Center; Mesa, Arizona; Mesa Arts Center • Montage Resort and Spa; Laguna Beach, California; The Athens Group • **Prudential Center Redevelopment**; Boston, Massachusetts; Boston Properties

Inc. • Stapleton District 1; Denver, Colorado; Forest City Enterprises • The Presidio Trust Management Plan; San Francisco, California; The Presidio Trust • Victoria Gardens; Rancho Cucamonga, California; Forest City Commercial Development and Lewis Group of Companies • Washington Convention Center; Washington, D.C.; Washington Convention Center Authority

2006 Europe
Agbar Tower; Barcelona, Spain; Layetana Developments • Muziekgebouw aan 't IJ; Amsterdam, The Netherlands; Dienst Maatschappelikjke Ontwikkeling • **New Milan Fair Complex**; Milan, Italy; Fondazione Fiera Milan • Potsdamer Platz Arkaden; Berlin, Germany; ECE Projektmanagement GmbH • Tour CBX; Paris la Défense, France; Tishman Speyer

2006 Asia Pacific
Glentrees; Singapore; CapitaLand Residential Singapore • Izumi Garden; Tokyo, Japan; Sumitomo Realty and Development Company Ltd. • Luohu Land Port and Train Station; Shenzhen, China; Shenzhen Municipal Planning Bureau • **Singapore Conservation Programme**; Singapore; Singapore Urban Redevelopment Authority • Wuxi Li Lake Parklands; Wuxi, China; Wuxi Lake District Planning & Construction Leading Team Office

2007 The Americas
1180 Peachtree; Atlanta, Georgia; Hines • 2200; Seattle, Washington; Vulcan Inc. • THE ARC; Washington, D.C.; Building Bridges Across the River • Daniel Island; Charleston, South Carolina; The Daniel Island Company • The Gerding Theater at the Armory; Portland, Oregon; Portland Center Stage • **High Point**; Seattle, Washington; Seattle Housing Authority • Highlands' Garden Village; Denver, Colorado; Perry Rose LLC and Jonathan Rose Companies • King's Lynne; Lynn, Massachusetts; King's Lynne Residents Council and Corcoran Mullins Jennison Inc. • RAND Corporation Headquarters; Santa Monica, California; The RAND Corporation • San Diego Ballpark Neighborhood Revitalization; San Diego, California; San Diego Padres, JMI Realty Inc., Bosa Development, Cisterra Partners LLC, and Douglas Wilson Companies • **Urban Outfitters Corporate Campus**; Philadelphia, Pennsylvania; Urban Outfitters Inc. (owner) Philadelphia Industrial Development Corporation (developer)

2007 Europe
Manufaktura; Łódź, Poland; Group Apsys • **Meudon Campus**; Meudon sur Seine, France; Hines • Kanyon; Istanbul, Turkey; Eczacibasi Holding • Petit Palau; Barcelona, Spain; Fundació Orfeó Català-Palau de la Música Catalana • Terminal 4 at Madrid Barajas Airport; Madrid-Barajas, Spain; AENA Aeropuertos Españoles y Navegación Aérea

2007 Asia Pacific
The Ecovillage at Currumbin; Currumbin, Queensland, Australia; Landmatters Currumbin Valley Property Ltd. • **Hong Kong Wetland Park**; Hong Kong, China; Architectural Services Department • The Landmark Scheme; Hong Kong, China; Hongkong Land • Nihonbashi Mitsui Tower; Tokyo, Japan; Mitsui Fudosan Co. Ltd. • Roppongi Hills; Tokyo, Japan; Mori Building Co. Ltd.

2008 The Americas
Adidas Village; Portland, Oregon; adidas-Salomon North America and Winkler Development Corporation • Army Residential Communities Initiative; U.S.A.-wide; U.S. Department of the Army • Atelier|505; Boston, Massachusetts; The Druker Company, Ltd. • Clipper Mill; Baltimore, Maryland; Struever Bros. Eccles & Rouse • Eleven80; Newark, New Jersey; Cogswell Realty Group •

General Motors Renaissance Center; Detroit, Michigan; General Motors and Hines • Medinah Temple-Tree Studios; Chicago, Illinois; Friedman Properties, Ltd. • National Ballet School of Canada/Radio City; Toronto, Canada; National Ballet School of Canada and Context Development, Inc. • Overture Center for the Arts; Madison, Wisconsin; Overture Development Corporation • Solara; Poway, California; Community Housing Works

2008 Europe
Kraanspoor; Amsterdam, The Netherlands; ING Real Estate Development • Meydan Shopping Square; Istanbul, Turkey; METRO Group Asset Management Gmbh & Co. • Stadsfeestzaal; Antwerp, Belgium; Multi Development Belgium nv • Unilever House; London, United Kingdom; Stanhope PLC and Sloane Blackfriars • Val d'Europe Downtown District; Marne la Vallée, France; Euro Disney Associes SCA, Value Retail PLC, Ségécé, and Nexity SA

2008 Asia Pacific
Beijing Finance Street; Beijing, China; Beijing Financial Street Holding Co., Ltd. • Bras Basah.Bugis; Singapore; Singapore; Urban Redevelopment Authority • Elements at Kowloon Station; Hong Kong, China; MTR Corporation Limited • The Kirinda Project; Kirinda, Sri Lanka; Colliers International Trust • Tokyo Midtown; Tokyo, Japan; Mitsui Fudosan Group

2009 The Americas
Baltimore Inner Harbor; Baltimore, Maryland; The Mayor, City Council of Baltimore and Charles Center-Inner Harbor Management, Inc. • California Academy of Sciences; San Francisco, California; California Academy of Sciences • Comcast Center; Philadelphia, Pennsylvania; Liberty Property Trust • The Cork Factory; Pittsburgh, Pennsylvania; McCaffery Interests, Inc. • DeVries Place; Milpitas, California; Mid-Peninsula Housing Coalition • Heifer International World Headquarters; Little Rock, Arkansas; Heifer International • Kansas City Power & Light District; Kansas City, Missouri; Cordish Company • Kierland Commons; Scottsdale, Arizona; Woodbine Southwest Corporation • The Rise; Vancouver, British Columbia, Canada; Grosvenor Americas • UniverCity; Burnaby, British Columbia, Canada; SFU Community Trust • West Chelsea/High Line Rezoning Plan; New York, New York; City of New York, Department of Planning

2009 EMEA
Akaretler Row Houses/W Hotel; Istanbul, Turkey; Akaretler Turizm Yatirimlari A.Ş. • American University in Cairo New Campus; Cairo, Egypt; AUC • Elmpark Green Urban Quarter; Dublin, Ireland; Radora Developments Ltd. • Hilton Tower; Manchester, United Kingdom; The Beetham Organization • Leoben Judicial Complex; Leoben, Austria; BIG Services • Liverpool One; Liverpool, United Kingdom; Grosvenor • Mountain Dwellings; Copenhagen, Denmark; Hoepfner and Danish Oil Company

2009 Asia Pacific
Crowne Plaza Changi Airport; Singapore; LaSalle Investment Management; L.C. Development Ltd. • Namba Parks; Osaka, Japan; Nankai Electric Railway Co. Ltd.; Takashimaya Company Ltd. • Seismically Resistant Sustainable Housing; Bagh and Jareed, Pakistan; Article 25 • Zhongshan Shipyard Park; Zhongshan, China; City of Zhongshan

Project names in red indicate ULI Heritage Award winners.

Project names in blue indicate ULI Global Award for Excellence winners.

2009 ULI GLOBAL AWARDS FOR EXCELLENCE

The ULI Global Awards for Excellence recognize projects that provide the best cross-regional lessons in land use practices. Up to five global winners may be named each year—chosen from among the year's 20 winners in the Americas, Europe, Middle East, and Africa (EMEA), and Asia Pacific—by a select jury of international members.

In 2009, there were five global winners, which were announced November 6 at the ULI Fall Meeting in San Francisco.

Because the Global Awards jury considers only projects that have been judged to have met ULI's criteria for an Award for Excellence, the jury bases its award determination on how projects meet the following standards:

- Establishing innovative concepts or standards for development that can be emulated around the world;
- Showing strong urban design qualities;
- Responding to the context of the surrounding environment;
- Exemplifying, where applicable, universally desirable principles of development, such as sustainability, environmental responsibility, pedestrian-friendly design, smart growth practices, and development around transit; and
- Demonstrating relevance to the present and future needs of the community in which they are located.

Winners of the 2009 Global Awards for Excellence

THE AMERICAS

California Academy of Sciences
San Francisco, California
Owner: California Academy of Sciences

Jury Statement: One of the world's largest LEED-Platinum public buildings, the $488 million California Academy of Sciences houses an aquarium, planetarium, natural history museum, and four-story rain forest. The 412,000-square-foot (38,300-m²) project, located in San Francisco's Golden Gate Park, was designed with the goal of preserving the natural habitats, species, and resources of the local environment.

West Chelsea/High Line Rezoning Plan
New York, New York

Owner: City of New York, Department of Planning

Jury Statement: Using an innovative transfer of development rights scheme, this plan has spurred the development of over 1,000 residential units and 2 million square feet (185,800 m²) of commercial space in West Chelsea. The defining feature of the special district is High Line Park—formerly an abandoned elevated rail line—which will become a 22-block-long linear park running through the district.

The Global Awards Jury

The chairman of ULI appoints the jury, which consists of five distinguished land use development and design practitioners. The chair of ULI's Policy and Practice Committee serves as the jury's chair. The other members are the chairs—or designees—of the three regional juries for Awards for Excellence and an at-large appointee. The 2009 Global Awards jury comprised the following members:

Joe Brown, Jury Chair, *group chief executive, AECOM, San Francisco, California*
Marilee Utter, *president, Citiventure Associates LLC, Denver, Colorado*
Raj Menda, *managing director, RMZ Corp, Bangalore, India*
Ian D. Hawksworth, *managing director, Capital & Counties, London, United Kingdom*
Richard Gollis, *principal, The Concord Group, Newport Beach, California*

The Rise
Vancouver, British Columbia, Canada

Owners/Developer: Grovesnor Americas

Jury Statement: The Rise, a mid-rise building adjacent to a rapid-transit station, successfully mixes large-format retail uses, locally focused stores, and 92 rooftop live/work units that surround a 20,000-square-foot (1,860-m²) green roof. The building uses one-third less energy and two-thirds less potable water than required by Canadian energy code, while the design establishes a new model of mixed-use development in Vancouver.

EMEA

American University in Cairo, New Campus
Cairo, Egypt
Owner/Developer: AUC

Jury Statement: The university's new campus is located at the center of New Cairo City, about 40 kilometers (25 mi) east of the current campus in downtown Cairo. It is designed to be a tool and stimulus in itself for learning and to anchor community development around the university. The 105-hectare (260-ac) virgin desert site has been developed into 200,000 square meters (2.2 million sf) of energy-efficient housing and academic, administrative, and student life facilities.

ASIA PACIFIC

Zhongshan Shipyard Park
Zhongshan, China

Owner/Developer: *City of Zhongshan*

Jury Statement: Built on a dilapidated shipyard, the Zhongshan Shipyard Park is 11 hectares (27 ac) of reclaimed wetlands, restored shoreline, and landscaped park space that references its industrial past with salvaged docks and machinery. The design gives much attention to restoring leftover structures, connecting with the existing urban context, and exercising environmental responsibility.

PHOTOGRAPHS BY TIM GRIFFITH (108); NEW YORK CITY DEPARTMENT OF PLANNING (109T); IAC INTERACTIVE CORP (109B); LARRY GOLDSTEIN (110T, 110B); ASHRAF SALLOUM (111T, 111B); KONGJIAN YU/CAO YANG (112T, 112B)